Designing Mobile Payment Experiences

Principles and Best Practices for Mobile Commerce

Skip Allums

 Beijing · Cambridge · Farnham · Köln · Sebastopol · Tokyo

Designing Mobile Payment Experiences
by Skip Allums

Copyright © 2014 Melford W. Allums, III. All rights reserved.

Printed in the United States of America.

Published by O'Reilly Media, Inc.,
1005 Gravenstein Highway North, Sebastopol, CA 95472.

O'Reilly books may be purchased for educational, business, or sales promotional use. Online editions are also available for most titles (*safari. oreilly.com*). For more information, contact our corporate/institutional sales department: (800) 998-9938 or *corporate@oreilly.com*.

Editor: Mary Treseler	**Cover Designer:** Ellie Volckhausen
Production Editor: Kara Ebrahim	**Interior Designers:** Ron Bilodeau and Monica Kamsvaag
Copyeditor: Rachel Monaghan	
Proofreader: Becca Freed	**Illustrator:** Rebecca Demarest
Indexer: Ginny Munroe	**Compositor:** Kara Ebrahim

August 2014: First Edition.

Revision History for the First Edition:

2014-08-04   First release

See *http://www.oreilly.com/catalog/errata.csp?isbn=0636920029816* for release details.

ISBN: 978-1-4493-6619-3

[LSI]

[Contents]

[*Preface*]

What Is This Book About?

As mobile devices emerge as tools for transacting and self-identifying, designers face challenging new interactions and user expectations, especially from payment scenarios. Consumers expect mobile payment experiences to be frictionless and familiar while faithfully protecting their financial data. Falling short on either of these aspects will cause users to drop out, or worse, will compromise their financial privacy. This book will show designers and developers how to meet these challenges through user experience (UX) best practices, as well as provide a primer on the world of mobile commerce.

What Are Mobile Payments?

When defining generally what a mobile payment is, I find it helpful to start by looking at *who is paying whom*, rather than delineating these experiences according to the facilitating technology (we'll get into that later). There are four basic categories, as outlined in Table P-1.

Of these four, this book focuses on consumer payments, though we will touch on the other three scenarios when appropriate. We'll talk about both in-person (standing inside a brick-and-mortar store) or remote (placing an order to pick up later) experiences. One reason for focusing on the consumer experience is sheer numbers: there are more mobile users who are consumers than those who are merchants. The other reason is that of these four scenarios, the act of making a purchase is the most nuanced and prone to ambiguity, and therefore the most challenging.

TABLE P-1. Basic categories of mobile payments

TYPE	DESCRIPTION	EXAMPLES
Consumer payments	Paying a merchant for goods or services	Starbucks, Isis Wallet
Merchant payments	Receiving money in exchange for goods or services from a consumer	Square Register, PayPal Here
Person-to-person payments	Sending money to another person, as a gift or a payback	Venmo, Dwolla
Institutional payments	Paying an institution for a monthly utility bill or debt	Check, Mobilligy

I may tackle the other three payment categories in future editions of this book. Merchant payments in particular would warrant a whole *series* (have you ever seen or used a point-of-sale terminal, pre-Square and the like? Yikes). At any rate, the tenets and recommendations I've included in this book, particularly those around ease of use and fostering user trust, could readily be applied to any sort of mobile commerce interaction.

Who Should Read This Book?

The audience for this book is designers, developers, and product managers interested in building a mobile commerce experience. I hope this book serves as a primer for experience makers from a variety of environments—from maverick startups looking to change the way we use our phones to those entrenched in the world of banking who are looking to integrate a new payment capability into their existing mobile services. This book started off as a simple list of mobile design principles, tailored for transactional experiences, which I kept for my own reference. I hope you will find it inspirational and instructive.

How This Book Is Organized

This book is organized into the following seven chapters:

Chapter 1, Bovines, Banknotes & Bytes
 A look back at the history of money and how humans pay for things, why this shapes user expectations and intentions, and how the intimate exchange between consumer and merchant has evolved.

e Money Ecosystem

the components of the mobile payments ecosys-
ese players work (or don't work) together to support
technologies.

'S Mobile Payment Experiences

tion of the current market of payment apps (Google
are, PayPal, LevelUp, and others), highlighting the
innovations and shortcomings of their designs.

Chapter 4, *Building Trust into Mobile Payments*
>   The first encounter with a payments app is fraught with peril: awk-
>   ward credit card form fields, endless legal disclaimers, and tricky
>   authentication flows. This chapter will demonstrate how to pain-
>   lessly onboard new users, while maintaining bank-grade security
>   and risk prevention.

Chapter 5, *Designing Successful Payment Interactions*
>   A walkthrough of the crux of this new paradigm...using a phone
>   at the point of sale to authorize a transaction. This chapter covers
>   many of the outcomes that could happen in the midst of a payment:
>   How does the user know when the payment is complete? What if
>   the transaction fails? What if the user needs to enter a PIN code?

Chapter 6, *Adding Value with Peripheral Services*
>   There are several value propositions that designers could miss,
>   which could progress a mobile payment experience from a novelty
>   to an essential. A mobile wallet can do things your old leather wal-
>   let can't do: send you discounts and deals for your favorite retail-
>   ers, help you track your spending and stick to a budget, complete
>   peer-to-peer money transfers, and get an updated balance on your
>   accounts.

Chapter 7, *Payments on the Horizon*
>   A look ahead at how these consumer experiences will shape the
>   retail and m-ecommerce world, and the emerging technologies
>   that will propel them.

Safari® Books Online

Safari Books Online (*http://my.safaribooksonline.com*) is an on-demand digital library that delivers expert *content* in both book and video form from the world's leading authors in technology and business. Technology professionals, software developers, web designers, and business and creative professionals use Safari Books Online as their primary resource for research, problem solving, learning, and certification training.

Safari Books Online offers a range of *product mixes* and pricing programs for *organizations, government agencies,* and *individuals.* Subscribers have access to thousands of books, training videos, and prepublication manuscripts in one fully searchable database from publishers like O'Reilly Media, Prentice Hall Professional, Addison-Wesley Professional, Microsoft Press, Sams, Que, Peachpit Press, Focal Press, Cisco Press, John Wiley & Sons, Syngress, Morgan Kaufmann, IBM Redbooks, Packt, Adobe Press, FT Press, Apress, Manning, New Riders, McGraw-Hill, Jones & Bartlett, Course Technology, and dozens *more.* For more information about Safari Books Online, please visit us *online.*

How to Contact Us

Please address comments and questions concerning this book to the publisher:

O'Reilly Media, Inc.

1005 Gravenstein Highway North

Sebastopol, CA 95472

800-998-9938 (in the United States or Canada)

707-829-0515 (international or local)

707-829-0104 (fax)

We have a web page for this book, where we list errata, examples, and any additional information. You can access this page at:

http://bit.ly/mobile-payment-ex

To comment or ask technical questions about this book, send email to:

bookquestions@oreilly.com

For more information about our books, courses, conferences, and news, see our website at *http://www.oreilly.com.*

Find us on Facebook: *http://facebook.com/oreilly*

Follow us on Twitter: *http://twitter.com/oreillymedia*

Watch us on YouTube: *http://www.youtube.com/oreillymedia*

Acknowledgments

This book would not have been possible without the boundless love and support of my beautiful wife, Sabrina, who put up with my late nights and general absentmindedness about anything not mobile commerce–related (parenting, household chores, personal hygiene, basic conversation skills) for the better part of a year while I wrote this book. To my giggly and bright baby boy, Miles, I am thankful that at six months you figured out how to sleep for 10 hours at a time, giving me a reliable daily window to write this book. I am looking forward to sketching and building new things with you, and helping you see our world filtered through your own creativity.

I'm thankful to my Mom for teaching me to approach any problem from all angles, not just how a textbook prescribes it (an uncommon view, coming from an algebra teacher). She also instilled in me the core values of Southern Hospitality, which influenced my own personal stamp on user experience design: courtesy, grace, and inclusion. I am grateful also to my Dad for teaching me that the best way to figure something out is to get your hands dirty, and to always pay attention to the details.

I am indebted to the impeccable staff at O'Reilly for helping me bring this book to life. In particular, I'd like to thank Mary Treseler, for putting the whole crazy idea in my head in the first place and then shaping that idea into a viable narrative. Amy Jollymore had the arduous task of slogging through each chapter to make some sense of the ramblings of a first-time writer. I thank you both for your guidance throughout this process. My first window into the world of user experience design was framed by great O'Reilly titles like *Information Architecture for the World Wide Web* and *Designing Web Interfaces*, so it is humbling for me to contribute to the wealth of knowledge available from this community.

I've been blessed with the tutelage of a few visionary mentors who have had a huge impact on my understanding of design for mobile financial services. My first design manager, Evan Gerber, instilled in me a holistic view of UX and how it fits into a person's daily life, as well as the ability to be creative under seemingly insurmountable design constraints. Evan is also responsible for stealing me away from the world of library and information science, and helped me to connect the dots from what I learned from that discipline to the broader needs of all technology users. I am also endlessly appreciative of my managers at Monitise, Stuart Cook and Chris Craver, for imparting decades of wisdom from their expertise in the world of financial technology, as well as for looking through early drafts to check my facts and offer feedback on the evolution of payments technology.

Lastly, I am thankful for the illuminating feedback from my early reviewers—Evan Gerber, Matthew Russell, and Tommy Wolber—for sharing their insight and sense-checking the material from the perspective of a wider tech and design audience. It's humbling to have input from some of the brightest minds in the industry.

But Wait...There's More

The world of technology is always in flux, and this is especially true in financial tech. I encourage you to visit my blog on mobile payments design to see my take on these emerging experiences through the eye of UX, and to share your views on this fascinating topic: *http://mobilepaymentux.com.*

[1]

Bovines, Banknotes & Bytes

We tend to think of money as a mundane artifact, either in digital or tangible form, that we employ to get the things we want. It is a means to an end. For example:

> I want a box of Twinkies.
> I have a credit card.
> I walk to the store, pick up a box from the snack aisle, and swipe my card.
> Now, I've got Twinkies!

Easy, right? And sinfully delicious!

But *why* do we expect payments to be so *easy?* The circulation and settlement of these funds are accomplished behind-the-scenes by a complex web of protocols and institutions, but we only ever see the tip of the iceberg that makes our daily purchases possible. Speedy transactions are a consumer expectation that has been *learned* over the thousands of years we have been purchasing things, and so digital experiences in this space must facilitate easy exchanges in kind.

Primarily, financial apps should be simple and intuitive. Payments with a mobile phone have to be as fast and reliable as cash or cards, because we are already accustomed to making payments several times a day with various methods: cards, cash, the Web, and others. We expect instant gratification from these exchanges. We have become familiar with these payment methods and they have proven to be successful over time, superseding other forms (checks) that fade into obsolescence. As financial paradigms have changed throughout the centuries, the idea of what currency ultimately *is* has become more abstract. Within this evolution, designers in this space should look beyond the tangible aspects of a payment instrument to gauge success, and focus on wider value and practicality surrounding the payment as a *system*. I have found that in order for a payment system to gain prominence and endure in the consumer mindset, it needs to embody three basic traits:

Convenience
> The medium of exchange must be practical, easy to handle, and easy to transport from the buyer to the seller. Historically, this aspect has been the driver of change as we seek ever-faster forms of payment.

Worth
> It must have an established and measurable store of value, which is apparent to all parties involved in the transaction.

Stability
> Before consumers even enter a store, they must have faith that their chosen payment method will be widely accepted, and maintain its worth and usefulness day after day.

Now, I don't claim to be an economist or a cultural anthropologist, but in this chapter we will take a look at some historical developments in payment mediums through the lens of these three traits. To appreciate how our concepts of money have evolved, we should first look back to simpler times (Figure 1-1).

Convenience

A Long Walk to the Market

> It's the year 3050 BC. One dark morning, near what is now Dunning in western Scotland, a farmer is walking two of his cows down a muddy path along the River Earn. It had rained all night, which is typical on this side of the river, but the late September sun is beginning to peek through the low clouds. The cows' long black hair is beaded with raindrops, and the farmer's heavy steps sink in the valleys of water pooled in the rutted road. He is on his way to a settlement where the Earn joins the River Tay, near modern-day Perth. There's an abrupt tug on the rope, as one cow stops to sniff the air. The farmer welcomes this reprieve. He's walked this road twice this season, and with Samhain fast approaching, this will likely be his last excursion to the market before winter sets in.

6000 BC — Commerce is accomplished with bartering of goods, or with commodities like livestock & crops within a community

2500 BC — Silver ingots and shekels, representing grain stores used as currency by the Mesopotamians

First electrum coins minted in Lydia, Turkey — **7th Century**

Chinese Song Dynasty begin circulating paper money — **11th Century**

Banks in Florence issue gold florins — **13th Century**

1717 — Bank of England produces first standardized paper check forms

The gold-backed US dollar is created by the US Mint — **1792**

1950 — Hamilton Credit Corporation creates Diner's Club charge card for member restaurants

1958 — Bank of America creates the BankAmericard, which becomes Visa in 1977

1971 — First magnetic stripe credit cards go into production at IBM

Europay, Mastercard and Visa (EMV) publish specifications for smart chip payments — **1996**

Confinity attempts mobile money transfers between Palm Pilots, later becomes PayPal — **1998**

2004 — First mobile NFC payment pilots in Japan and South Korea in transit stations and vending machines

2006 — M-PESA becomes popular in Kenya, allowing unbanked to pay bills, make deposits and transfer money on USSD feature phones. Within 3 years, expands to South Africa and India

Figure 1-1. A timeline of a few key developments in payment systems

He hopes to trade the cows for supplies that will get his family through the cold gray months, like oil for lamps, or wool for heavy blankets and clothing. He is especially looking forward to picking up some salted salmon, caught off St. Andrews by his wife's cousin. If all goes well at market, at noon he can start the four-hour trek back home before dark.

It is difficult for us to imagine now, but this is an example of what might have been a typical shopping trip in early Western civilization. The farmer hopes that each local producer (the fisherman, the shepherd) will accept one cow in exchange for the goods he seeks: oil and wool from the shepherd, salmon from the fisherman. The farmer must rely on mutual trust that goods he is seeking are available in his community, and of good quality. He trades with the same vendors over a sustained period of time, and they become like extended family. These types of intimate interactions fostered community interdependence, and gave rise to the first markets.

BARTERING AND THE BIRTH OF CURRENCY

Though we may never know *when* humans began to exchange goods, it is likely that neighborly favors and *bartering* (one-to-one trade of goods and services understood to be of equal value) was no doubt the starting point. Bartering eventually gave way to the rise of agriculture as a type of currency, as our communities grew larger and more prosperous. For example, farmers would raise more cattle than they needed for their own families, and then trade the extra cattle with nearby producers for other necessities, such as fish, animal fat for fuel, or sheep's wool for clothing (Figure 1-2). Towns sprung up around crossroads, and routes were carved out to link culturally isolated populations—all to enable the trading of commodities.[1] Bartering and commodity exchange was effective for simple transactions between two parties for goods perceived as equal in value. However, these exchanges were subject to timeliness or need, and so would lead to inconvenient redundancies. What if the fisherman had no need for more cattle? What if the shepherd had no rendered oil to spare? What if the shepherd felt that one cow was not as valuable as a bundle of wool? The farmer would have to hit the road to find other producers to trade with who needed what he was offering, or otherwise take the long walk home empty-handed.

---

1 Jack Weatherford, *The History of Money* (New York: Three Rivers Press, 1997), 93.

Figure 1-2. Woodcut by Olaus Magnus, depicting the trading of tools, weapons, fish, and grain by 16th-century Nordic peoples[2]

To address this, the concept of credit, and later of shared currencies, emerged in order to serve a logistical need for efficient commerce. From 2500 BC with the Mesopotamian *shekel* to the 12th-century *hui-zi* paper notes of the Song Dynasty, cultures around the world began to develop more convenient mechanisms to enable trade. Our farmer's descendants likely relied on local, familiar merchants who knew them and would extend to them a line of credit, kept in the form of a written ledger, which could then be repaid in time with commodities or favors. By the time the Romans arrived in Britain, they would have begun paying with coins or other tokens, which were *much* easier to transport than two wet bovines, and were widely accepted by other members of his community.

All coins, big and small

The first coins would have been made from a malleable metal like silver or bronze, and stamped with the sigils of the local lord or Roman gods (Figure 1-3). Our friend the farmer could sell his two cows in the market for *five* coins, which he could take to the shepherd and the fisherman to pick up his supplies, and perhaps have one or two coins left over for savings (and, of course, taxes). The portability of coins contributed to their popularity across cultures, and they worked so well that we still use them to this day.

---

2 Olaus Magnus, *History of the Nordic Peoples, On Trade Without Using Money*, vol. 4, chapter 5 (1555).

Figure 1-3. Lydian coins from 575 BC were some of the first to be minted at a consistent purity and mass (courtesy of Kwan Choi, Iowa State University)

Not all coins are so practical. One favorite story of financial nerds and currency anthropologists is from the island of Yap in the Western Pacific (between Guam and the Philippines), where the exchange of *rai* stones (Figure 1-4) gained prevalence 2,000 years ago. The rai ranged in size from small limestone beads to massive, 12-foot-wide wheels.[3] Being impossibly impractical, they are used today in only ceremonial exchanges (e.g., weddings, political events, and estate transfers), and they are not usually moved from their bases. Rai coins didn't propagate as a day-to-day currency due to their physical enormity, but we'll talk more about them as an example of understood *worth* later in this chapter.

---

3 William Henry Furness, *The Island of Stone Money* (Philadelphia: J. B. Lippincott & Co., 1910), 93 (*http://bit.ly/1j8XLaf*).

Figure 1-4. A rai stone coin, measuring about 12 feet in diameter (courtesy of Joshua Levin/Flickr [*http://bit.ly/1j8XVOS*])

Honey, I forgot my wallet

Let's move ahead several centuries to a similar invention, born out of the pursuit of convenience. The first charge cards came about due to the need to rely on a trusted network to enable cashless purchases. Charge plates, an early version of the charge card, were tin plates similar to military dog tags that became popular in the 1920s and 30s (Figure 1-5).[4] They were stamped with the name and address of the cardholder, who at the time of purchase could simply hand over the charge plate to the cashier, who would in turn imprint the plate onto a bill of sale. The raised lettering of charge plates has carried over to modern-day credit cards, though it is rare to find a card-imprinting slider at today's point of sale (unless the power goes out). Charge plates were issued to the most frequent and loyal customers of department stores and gas stations, to enable them to put purchases on a tab that could be settled up monthly.

---

4   Scott B. MacDonald and Albert L. Gastmann, *A History of Credit & Power in the Western World* (Piscataway, NJ: Transaction Publishers, 2004), 227.

Figure 1-5. A charge plate belonging to Mrs. Ira B. Zasloff—note the stylish leather case! (courtesy of Ron Toth Jr., 2013)

This meant that customers didn't have to carry large amounts of cash if they wanted to purchase a dining set or a washing machine. There was an air of prestige associated with charge plates, as they implied that one had the sort of income that would make one a frequent shopper at Bloomingdale's or Saks Fifth Avenue. Still, it's hard to imagine now having to carry around half a dozen tin plates in your wallet: one for each of your favorite stores.

That is when one of the predecessors of the modern general-purpose credit card entered the scene: the Diners Club card (Figure 1-6). In 1950, Frank McNamara's Hamilton Credit Corporation issued the Diners Club card: a printed cardboard card that could be used at 14 participating New York City restaurants. The legend was that McNamara forgot his wallet one night during a business dinner and had to call his wife to bail him out, and he swore never again to be without an alternate way to pay for his tab (though this story may have been a myth created by McNamara's business partner, Alfred Bloomingdale).

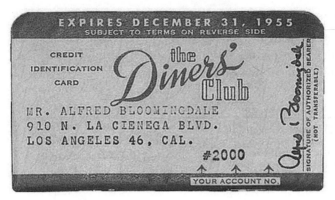

Figure 1-6. Alfred Bloomingdale's Diners Club card (courtesy of Diners Club, 1954)

When the waiter handed you the bill at dinner, you would hand over the card, sign, and the bill would be added to your tab, which had to be paid in full each month. Diner's Club skyrocketed in popularity, adding 20,000 cardholders and 1,000 restaurants in five major US cities within its first year.[5] This was the first time a membership charge card could be used ubiquitously (at least for fine dining); most charge cards were accepted only at the individual retailers who issued them.

This "charge where I want" concept soon became the norm with credit cards, as large national banks got behind it (small regional banks had been providing charge cards since 1946) and began to issue their own cards to their customers. Bank of America's BankAmericard launched in 1958 and would go on to become Visa.[6] MasterCharge (later MasterCard) launched in 1969, formed by a consortium of banks including Wells Fargo, HSBC, and Union Bank of California.[7] Augmented by the magnetic stripe and later the smart chip, plastic credit and debit cards made it effortless to make cashless purchases (for better or for worse). Execution of these card swipes is carried out via a system (Figure 1-7) that takes the cardholder's account information and passes it from the merchant to the merchant's bank to the card network (Visa, MasterCard, American Express, etc.) to the bank that issued the

5 Diners Club International website, "About Diners Club: The Story Behind the Card" (http:// bit.ly/1j8Y6cZ).

6 Visa Inc. website, "History of Visa" (http://vi.sa/1j8YjwR).

7 MasterCard website, "About Us" (http://bit.ly/1j8Yo3A).

card to check for sufficient funds. Then, the issuing bank gives a positive authorization response back to the merchant's bank (via the card network), which then notifies the merchant that the card is valid. All this back-and-forth takes just a few seconds.

Authorization

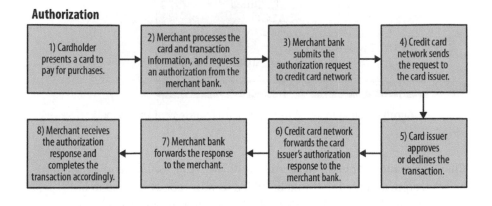

Clearing and Settlement

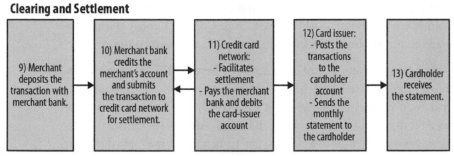

Figure 1-7. How a credit card payment works (courtesy of UniBul Merchant Services);[8] it's amazing that so many confirmations are communicated within seconds of swiping your card!

Now, of course, plastic cards are ubiquitous. In 2008, at the lowest point of the recession, the Federal Reserve of Boston conducted a survey of consumer payment habits. It found that 77% of US consumers use debit cards, and 72% have credit cards, with debit cards being the most preferred payment instrument, at an average of 19 purchases

8   UniBul Merchant Services, "Submission Clearing and Settlement of Credit Card Transactions" (*http://bit.ly/1j8Yvwb*).

a month.[9] Convenience drives popularity—consider that even in the middle of a recession, plastic cards were used for about three-fourths of all purchases.

With so many different ways to pay for things, we can now associate payment methods with different *tasks*. Like the charge plates a few decades before, it has become customary to have about six plastic cards in our wallets, each with a specific purpose: one for the gas station, one for travel, one for dining and entertaining, one for earning loyalty points, and so on.[10] Bills and rent could be paid with checks, or wired via transfer services like Western Union. Cash could be used for everyday purchases like groceries or tollbooths. Consumers are now free to establish their own preferences for particular payment methods, according to the context and ease of use.

PAYING WITH BYTES

The next time you visit your local shopping mall, stop for a minute and look around. Imagine you are a weary traveler, shopping at a 12th-century Roman market—they are not too dissimilar, after all. There is a busy central corridor, lined with merchants, each specializing in a particular inventory: clothing, food, jewelry, shoes, massage chairs, enormous cinnamon rolls, etc. What has changed (apart from the fashions in the windows)? Hardly anyone is using cash!

Our progression to a cashless society will be a slow but inevitable one. Today, about 80% of all payments (not just retail, but bills, too) in the US are done with cash,[11] and 29% of us are carrying around about 20 to 50 dollars' worth.[12] That amounts to a *lot* of dollar bills floating around. For some, all these bills and coins are more of a hassle than an asset. Cash is not especially safe to carry in large amounts, and you generally get it from ATMs, which aren't always around when you need them. Drawing cash from an ATM that is not provided by your bank will ding you with out-of-network fees. And there could be several *thousand*

---

9 Federal Reserve of Boston, "2009 Survey of Consumer Payment Choice" (*http://bit.ly/1j8YJmX*).

10 Ibid, 8.

11 MasterCard Advisors report, "Cashless Journey," 4 (*http://bit.ly/1j8YU1G*).

12 Bankrate.com Financial Security Index Survey, May 4, 2014 (*http://bit.ly/1j8YZ5J*).

harmful bacteria floating around on each bill—*blech!*[13] Coins have become a jingling annoyance, relegated to a glass jar as soon as we walk in our front doors, useful only for parking meters and laundromats. In 2013, the burden of carrying cash around sparked tense debates over the perceived redundancy of one of the most iconic US coins: the penny![14] Cash is familiar to us, of course, but is it worth the hassle? Technology has given us tools to avoid handling this clumsy, "dirty" money all together.

ANYTIME, ANYWHERE

As consumers are presented with digital methods for moving their money, how do these methods change how they pay for things? How have new financial technologies made their lives easier? What impact do these innovations have on how consumers manage and track their spending? Money is becoming more ethereal in nature...sometimes it's just a bunch of ones and zeros.

The ecommerce revolution extended the act of shopping to a new plane of utility. The Internet created a dynamic medium for retailers to advertise and sell their merchandise to customers. This allowed them to reach a broader market, and enabled consumers around the world to browse their shelves without being restricted by store hours. Web superstores like Amazon.com and eBay sell vast amounts of goods without the buyers and sellers ever speaking to each other. Brick-and-mortar chains like Walmart and Target have followed suit, providing their customers with the chance to shop without leaving the comfort of their couches.

The possibilities are limitless. You can shop for *anything* online: groceries from a chain supermarket, shoes from Italy, guayabera shirts from Guatemala, rare books from Montreal, bacon-flavored potato chips, turtleneck sweaters for your pug, and more. It's all at your fingertips, once you add your items to an online shopping cart and enter your credit card details.

---

13 MasterCard report, "How Clean Is Your Cash?", March 25, 2013 (*http://bit.ly/1j8Z6Ou*). "Independent research carried out by scientists at Oxford University reveals that European bank notes on average contain over 26,000 bacteria, with 2,400 bacteria found on the cleanest, newest currency." Yikes.

14 David Owen, "Please, Finally, End the Penny," *New York Times*, April 4, 2012 (*http://nyti. ms/1j8Z8Wq*).

Auction sites like eBay made the thrill of moonshot bidding a national sport. If your index finger is fast enough, you can scoop up that rare first-issue comic book you've been eyeing for years. Once your bank account is linked to PayPal, picking up discount items is a breeze. By 2000, 41 million Americans had begun purchasing products online.[15]

This comfort with transacting online spurred consumers to trust their financial information with more versatile web-based tools. In 1994, Stanford Federal Credit Union was the first to introduce online banking to its account holders, who were employees of Stanford University in Palo Alto, California (Figure 1-8). Its customers would go to the bank's website and encounter a virtual bank branch. They could check their balances, make transfers between accounts, and see their transaction history. Three years later, SFCU's customers could use electronic payments to pay their utility bills.

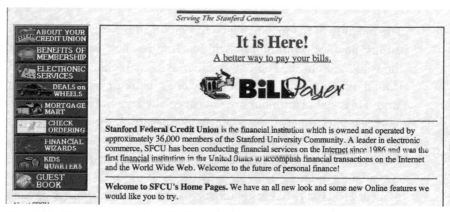

Figure 1-8. Stanford Federal Credit Union's website in 1997 (courtesy of Internet Archive)

By 2001, US banks had 31 million online customers.[16] As with Internet shopping, the convenience of banking from home was the biggest draw. In less time than it takes to brew a cup of coffee, bank customers could transfer money to their savings accounts or pay a bill from their home computers. Compare that with the amount of time and effort required

---

15 Pew Internet & American Life, Online Banking Survey, 2002 (*http://bit.ly/1j8Zht6*).
16 Ibid.

to conduct traditional banking tasks: getting in the car and driving to the local bank branch, standing in line for a teller, presenting an ID and bank account number, and filling out a form.

Consequently, our reliance on printed copies of our monthly account statements has waned, as has the use of paper in general. In 1995, the Federal Reserve processed 49.5 billion checks. By 2000, that number had dropped to 42.5 billion, while the number of people using online bill pay rose to 12 million households.[17] In 2009, the Federal Reserve released a study that painted a dark picture for the use of cash and checks. By that time, the volume of checks processed was down to $29.5 billion. Compare that with the volume of debit and credit card transactions, which came in at $59.5 billion.[18] Online banking was the perfect counterpart to this shift, as consumers could now track their spending by opening up their web browsers and sifting through their transaction histories.

The ubiquity of the mobile phone has changed the way we do a lot of things: how we communicate with each other, how we interact with the world around us, and how we manage our money. As we moved from desktops to laptops to mobile phones, banking has gravitated in kind. Financial institutions are not especially known for being behavioral "game changers," but when banks began powering our phones with the same services we can get on our laptops (account balances, transfers, bill pay, spending alerts), it became much harder to be ignorant of one's finances. The company I work for, Monitise, helped Royal Bank of Scotland (RBS) bring mobile banking to its customers' mobile devices in 2010. Within six months of launch, we saw that customers were checking their account balances 10 times a month, or about twice a week. In February 2014, RBS noted in its annual results that it had more than 2.5 million active mobile users using the service an average of 28 times a month.[19] Mobile banking enables us to manage our finances on the go, and feel more in control of our money.

---

17 Jean Chatzky, "The Check Is in the Mail. Not!," *Time*, October 14, 2002 (*http://ti.me/1j8ZsVk*).

18 2010 Federal Reserve Payments Study, Noncash Payment Trends in the United States: 2006–2009, 4 (*http://bit.ly/1j8ZCMl*).

19 RBS Annual Results 2013, February 27, 2014 (*http://bit.ly/1j8ZGLV*).

In some parts of the world with little (or no) financial infrastructure, mobile banking and payments has done more than allow people to bank with ease—it has proved capable of transforming entire economies. In 2007, mobile network operator Safaricom (a Vodafone company) launched the M-PESA service in Kenya (Figure 1-9), which enabled mobile money transfers and bill payments.[20] *Pesa* is Swahili for money, so the name of the service literally means "mobile money."

Figure 1-9. An M-PESA customer receives a text message that confirms the transfer of 4,300 Kenyan shillings from his account (courtesy of Peter Gakure-Mwangi, *http://www.thinkm-pesa.com/*)

Let's say you lived and worked in an urban center, and your parents lived in a rural area. In Kenya, before services like M-PESA came around, if you wanted to send money home to your family you would take your cash and hand it over to a taxi driver, or perhaps a friend who was taking the bus, and instruct him to take it to your parents' village.

---

20 Fiona Graham, "M-Pesa: Kenya's Mobile Wallet Revolution," BBC News, November 22, 2010 (*http://www.bbc.co.uk/news/business-11793290*).

Eventually (or maybe *never*), the bus or the taxi driver would arrive at the village and your mom or dad could pick up the cash. As you can imagine, this isn't a very secure or efficient system.

Unfortunately, many who live in rural areas do not have a bank account, or even access to a bank, which is what you traditionally need to securely transfer money between individuals. When M-PESA introduced mobile bill pay and money transfers, its customers began using the system to send money instantly to anywhere in the country. If the recipient also had an M-PESA-enabled phone, then the money would be credited to his account, which could be used to reload his prepaid account, pay bills, or exchange for cash at an M-PESA agent or ATM. If the recipient wasn't an M-PESA customer, he could still show the text message with the reference number of the payment at any of the 40,000 local M-PESA shops, and could receive cash. Access to the funds in an M-PESA account is protected by the user's four-digit PIN, used to authorize any transaction.

M-PESA launched in March 2007, and has grown incredibly: by March 2013 it had 17 million users.[21] M-PESA can be used not just for personal payments, but also for buying groceries, paying utility bills, or even paying taxi drivers. The success of M-PESA is a fine example of how the search for practicality and convenience has spurred payment systems to evolve within technological eras.

Worth

Looking back a few pages, why was it possible for those enormous rai stones on the island of Yap to *ever* function as a form of currency? They were way too heavy to carry around for everyday use, and you'd likely die if one fell on you. Despite being cumbersome, the rai stones gained intrinsic value within the Yap culture, due to the stones' makeup and rarity—there are no limestone deposits on Yap—but also the immense physical effort inherent in obtaining them. They were shipped in canoes from limestone quarries in the Palau Islands 280 miles away. Even if a rai stone fell into the sea during the trek (which happened

---

21 Safaricom Limited website, "Timeline of M-PESA: Celebrating 7 Years of Changing Lives" (*http://www.safaricom.co.ke/mpesa_timeline/timeline.html*).

quite often), the oral agreement between the exchanging parties could still stand, as the effort involved in mining, shaping, and transporting the stone was witnessed and verified by the community at large.

At the core of a transaction, the parties involved need to believe that exchanging a currency as a form of payment will result in the desired outcome: the consumer will receive the item she purchased, and the merchant will receive income from the sale. Time has shown us that this is possible regardless of the raw *substance* of the currency as an artifact. What matters is perceived *worth*. The merchant and the customer must trust that the currency—whether it is salt, shells, stones, coins, or digital blobs—will be recognized as *valuable* by others within their community, and that it will not soon fall out of favor. Historically, gold was an obvious choice, given that it does not rust and is easily shaped into any form. Paper was less obvious—it isn't beautiful or rare, but early in our history it became the de facto proxy for gold, grain, or other wealth held by the administrative entity who minted it. This was possible because paper could take on inferred value by the community that created and circulated it. Worth is the most abstract trait of a payment system, and so is most susceptible to flux due to factors like government instability, fraud, and public opinion.

INTRODUCING PAPER MONEY

In the year 1000 in Western China, commerce was blossoming. However, people were growing tired of juggling the currency of the day: hefty copper coins with square holes punched in them so that they could be strung together in long bands. They needed a form of currency that was easier to handle in large amounts. So, the merchant guilds experimented with paper notes they called *jiao-zi* or "exchange medium" as a kind of promissory note (Figure 1-10).[22]

---

22 F. W. Mote, *Imperial China: 900–1800* (Cambridge, MA: Harvard University Press, 2003), 364.

Figure 1-10. Jiao-zi paper notes, which were later minted by the Song Dynasty as hui-zi: the 10 circles on top represent the denomination in coins, and a market scene is depicted at the bottom, below the issuing merchant association's stamp (image courtesy of Ministry of Culture, P.R. China)

Using jiao-zi became so popular that the Song government took over the minting of the notes, which it renamed *hui-zi*. Each note could be exchanged for its corresponding value in copper coins. Hui-zi were block-stamped with the government seal and the denomination, as well as a warning to counterfeiters (punishment for printing fake bills was typically beheading). This happy experiment did not last, however, as the overprinting of the notes caused the value to drop drastically. Still, this practice persisted even after the Mongols had invaded the region in 1276, though they later minted and enforced their own distinct currencies. Paper was successful as a payment medium in this case because of its portability, as well as the regulation and distribution by a governing party.

LET'S TALK TURKEY

Still, *having* money alone isn't enough to spawn commerce. We have to get along with each other first. Parties on both sides have to speak a common language to establish a mutual trust that is then transferred onto the money being used. Aside from being basic economic "events" that are beneficial to the parties involved, what makes these exchanges so personal is that they are usually accompanied by humane gestures, even when strangers are transacting. Surely the merchants of the Song Dynasty did not all know each other *personally*, but there must have been a modicum of social grace that was observed before a transaction took place.

Today, most of our brick-and-mortar payments are initiated with cheerful greetings (aside from vending machine encounters). Even the largest big-box chain store is designed to exude helpfulness and approachability. At the door, we are met with a cheerful "How are you?" and asked if we "need help finding anything?" Items on the shelf are logically organized (hopefully), clearly labeled, and marked with price tags (Figure 1-11). These stimuli resonate just as deeply with users during a digital transaction.

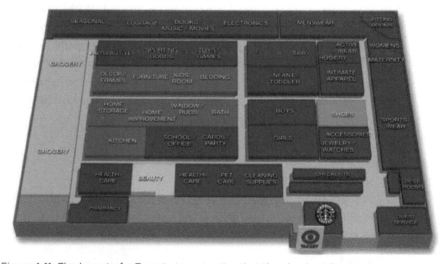

Figure 1-11. The layout of a Target store—notice that the checkout line, restrooms, and guest services are located near the front entrance, so that they are easy to find (courtesy of Target)

Financial interactions at their core are a conversation between buyer and seller. Just like in a conversation with a friend, we might have expectations relevant to the context of where the transaction takes place, the end goal of the transaction, as well as familiar language patterns and behavioral cues that will ensure that we (consumer and merchant) will reach our desired goals. This back-and-forth between consumer and merchant extends back to our earliest markets, where weighing the value of goods and haggling over the best price brought about rituals of commerce, and conversation as art. For example, if you were shopping in a 13th-century Moroccan *souk*, a ritual of greetings and tea drinking would precede a transaction. To skip straight to haggling would have been gauche, and the merchant may have chosen not to do business with you. Your social grace and reputation as a seller (or customer) would speak just as loudly as how many coins you had in your purse. These rituals ideally established good faith and relationships between the two parties, which transferred both to the goods purchased and the form of currency changing hands.

This tenet of mutual trust has persisted throughout the evolution of payment systems. In the early 1700s, there was a shortage of small change in England. The Bank of England's pound sterling was strong, but there weren't many smaller notes to go around. Within the City of London's financial hub, merchants began to write letters to their banker, authorizing the release of funds to a payee—usually in sums below £20. The merchant would give the letter, called a *drawn note*, to the person he intended to pay.[23] The drawn note could be redeemed for cash at the merchant's bank. These informal letters would mature into what we know now as the check.

A typical letter, as seen in Figure 1-12, would read like this:

> Mr. A Fowler,
> Pray you pay to Mr. Thomas Hill without further advice the sum of seventy pounds. —and this receipt shall be your sufficient discharge for the same—
>
> Signed,
>
> 9 October, 1725

---

23 Richard David Richards, *The Early History of Banking in England* (London: P. S. King and Son, Ltd., 1929), 50.

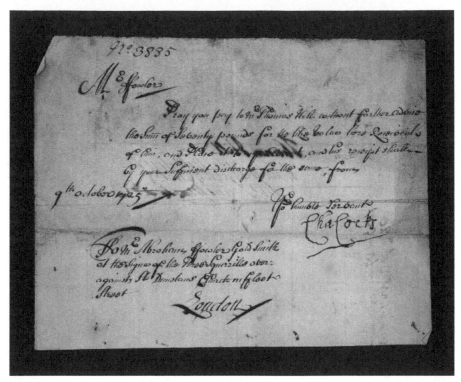

Figure 1-12. A drawn note, an early form of bank check, 1725—note the letter is addressed to Abraham Fowler, Goldsmith (a term for banker) on Fleet Street, London; Mr. Fowler's bank became Goslings & Company, one of the first branches of Barclays, and the Goslings branch still stands today at 19 Fleet Street (courtesy of British Museum)

Of course, this was not the first financial paper trail by any means. As early as the fourth millennium BC, the Sumerians were inscribing pictographic records of sales and debts in stone tablets. A letter like this was particularly handy if one was not in possession of enough cash to pay someone at a particular moment—say if you had borrowed cash from a friend to pay for a large expense that you could not cover on your own. Initiation of this sort of transaction required an establishment of faith among the three individuals: the account holder trusts his banker will store and release his funds at his bidding, the banker trusts his account holder to keep his accounts in good standing, and the payee trusts that the account holder is good for the money.

A NUMBERS GAME

So, what happens when there is no *physical* form of currency? These days, when you hear or read about a sum of money, say $100,000, what do you see in your mind? Do you picture stacks of hundred-dollar bills, or do you picture it as a number on a bank statement, or a green line item on the transaction history of an online banking site? The use of hard cash is dwindling as we shift to forms of payments like credit cards or electronic payment, where we never have to physically *handle* the money.

Money has become too easy to spend! With the tangibility of coins and paper bills, you are explicitly aware of how much money you are spending because you can see the money dwindle in your hands.[24] For example, say you started the week with $100. If you buy a t-shirt that costs $12, you will likely count out the paper bills to add up to the total, perhaps two $5s and two $1s, and hand it over to the merchant. Now you have $88 left in your wallet.

If you take away the dollar bills and instead use a plastic card to pay for the t-shirt, and then use that card again several times in a day, you might be less aware of exactly how much you are spending. To properly track your purchases and take stock of your personal financial status, you must rely on another information source, like a checkbook balance or a bank statement.

Even if you do see a record of your purchases on your bank statement, what you see there may not tell you what you really want to know. Paper bank statements are dumb lists, and are not great at telling you how much of your monthly budget has gone to dining out or to utility bills. One example of this is a confusing by-product of transaction records that renders most events on your bank statement into gobbledygook. For example, on this month's bank statement, I have the following transaction:

CHECK CRD PURCHASE 10/24 76 10098523
NAPA CA 41111111XXXXXX0590 ?MCC=5542 - $67.25

---

24 Dilip Soman, "The Effect of Payment Transparency on Consumption: Quasi-Experiments from the Field," *Marketing Letters* vol. 14, no.3 (2003): 173–183 (*http://bit.ly/1j9ojVZ*).

I can infer that on October 24th I used my debit card for something in Napa, California, possibly at a 76 gas station, that cost me $67.25, but not much else. That's not very helpful. The average consumer wouldn't be able to interpret much from this item. Since I happen to work with financial services clients, I know that MCC stands for Merchant Category Code, and that "MCC=5542" means the purchase was made at an "automated fuel dispenser." Now I can extrapolate that jumble of numbers and letters into something more meaningful, and add in plain-language descriptors to provide more context:

October 24, 2013
Merchant: 76 Gas Station, Store No. 10098523
Location: Napa, California
Total: $67.25
Paid with: Visa Debit Card ending ...0590

That's much easier to understand! Fortunately, a new generation of banking services is layering a more user-friendly sheen on typically dry banking interfaces. The scenario just described (giving context to transaction histories) is one of the selling points of Intuit's Mint (Figure 1-13). Once the user links her bank account to Mint, the app will begin to translate payment histories and statements into tables that are easier to sift through. Mint pulls out known merchant IDs and categories from these histories and populates helpful graphs to illustrate spending patterns. Mint also endeavors to help its users make smart financial decisions by enabling budget planning and goal setting. Once you set up a monthly budget profile, Mint can then show you a snappy graph that gives you a clear idea of where you stand on a daily basis.

Another service in this vein is Simple Bank (Figure 1-14). Although backed by a brick-and-mortar financial institution (FDIC-insured Bancorp), it has none of the cornflower-blue corporate branding, awkward web interfaces, and confusing service agreements. Simple is a web-only bank; it does not have physical bank branches. It issues customers a plain, "simple" white Visa debit card, and any purchases made with the card are tracked by the mobile app and online dashboard, where they are fed into visualizations of spending categories and monthly budgets.

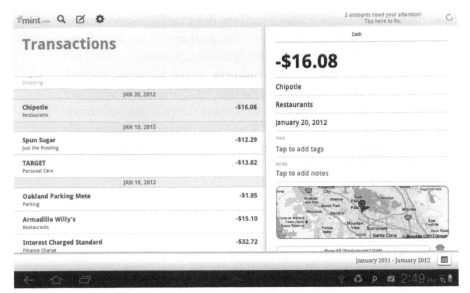

Figure 1-13. Mint.com offers rich transaction statements in plain English, as well as automatic and custom categorization (courtesy of Mint.com)

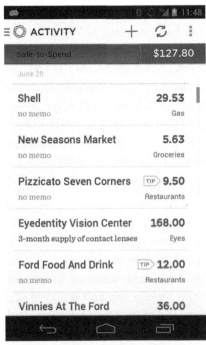

Figure 1-14. Simple Bank displays a prominent "safe-to-spend" balance that takes into account pending transactions, scheduled payments, and savings goals (courtesy of Simple.com)

On the Simple mobile app, your available balance is clearly displayed at the top of the screen—but instead of showing a running balance, which you would normally see when you ask for a balance from your bank, Simple takes into any account pending transactions *plus* recurring monthly payments you have scheduled, as well as deducting toward any savings goals you have set for yourself. This feature is meant to help you save money by preventing you from overspending, and to keep you aware of obligations and goals.

With time-saving features like mobile check deposit (taking a picture of a check to transmit a deposit to your bank account) or bill pay with automatic paper-check-mailing services, these new-generation banking applications are enabling today's consumers to stay on top of their spending, and putting cognitive weight back into digital money.

Stability

Payment systems thrive when they make the logistics of commerce more efficient, but also when the payment medium itself is perceived as being *reliable* in the eyes of those who are using it. This can be related to maintaining a consistent value over time, or being backed by an institution or by gold stores (such as paper money used to be). This sense of stability could be reinforced by the aesthetics of the payment artifact itself. These tangible and intangible factors combine to create an aura of general trustworthiness.

An example of a tangible factor could be how the payment artifact *looks*. Coin and bills are usually stamped with symbols from an official mint or regulating institution (Figure 1-15). Historically, this could have been images of the kings or lords whom we also trusted to protect our lands from invaders and uphold local laws. The coins just *looked* official (and counterfeiting was dissuaded by the consequence of death by especially unpleasant means). These images of institutional sponsorship carry over to today's banknotes and coins, emblazoned with the floating heads of state and symbols that draw on the collective sense of national pride.

Figure 1-15. An 1865 US banknote, a $10 bill printed by a bank in Rhode Island—note the patriotic symbolism of the eagle and Benjamin Franklin; before the Federal Reserve Act of 1913, regional banks could print their own currency (courtesy of the Frost Currency Collection, John Hay Library)

SEE ME, TOUCH ME, FEEL ME

How a currency looks can have a huge impact on its perceived worth. Let's face it: US paper money leaves much to be desired in terms of aesthetics, though it is one of the dominating forces of the world financial stage. For decades, our money has remained stoic in its olive-hued constancy, a gallery of grim presidential noggins staring back at you. My wife and I spent our honeymoon in Costa Rica. There, we were astounded at how truly *dull* our native currency is, once we got hold of Costa Rican *colónes*. Costa Rican bills are a pleasant mélange of golds, oranges, greens, and blues, with lifelike illustrations of local wildlife, historical leaders, and scenes of Costa Rica's abundant natural beauty (Figure 1-16). There are transparent windows carved into them, with insets of a map of the country or national symbols. The colón is a work of art, but its beauty belies its substance.

Costa Rica was actually the first country to print its bills on polymer.[25] The first plastic colónes were made of Tyvek sheets manufactured by DuPont. Polymer notes are not only extremely resilient, they are also hard to fake. They can be laden with all manner of magnetic security strips, RFID tags, watermarks, and micro-inks to dissuade counterfeiters. They can last 2.5 times longer than paper bills, being impervious

---

25 American Bank Note Company Annual Report, 1984 (*http://bit.ly/1j909xC*).

to washing machines and the jaws of family pets.²⁶ This is not your grandfather's $2 greenback! Now there are all these vibrant, colorful currencies floating around in consumers' pockets all over the world, and thankfully no one is carting sacks of grain around to pay his neighborhood grocer.

Figure 1-16. 20,000 Costa Rican colónes

Because the imagery on a banknote carries such immense cultural weight, it can have a profound effect on its stability as a currency. Designing interfaces for a new kind of payment app is one thing, but imagine having to build an entirely new *currency*—one that would be used by many nations! In 1996, the European Monetary Institute (EMI) had just that challenge. It held a design contest, and chose Austrian currency designer Robert Kalina's concept for the new Euro bank note.²⁷ EMI conducted a survey across the EU with a short list of submitted design concepts. Money handlers and consumers were shown mock bills and asked to weigh their various aspects (aesthetics, legibility, size). Kalina had chosen motifs of stately, recognizable icons of European architecture: pastoral window frames, stately bridges, and Roman aqueducts: "I came to this idea of bridges to symbolize

---

26 C. W., "What's the Point of Plastic Banknotes?", *The Economist*, November 13, 2013 (*http://econ.st/1j9oel3*).

27 Elizabeth Bryant, "Interview: Designer Bridges Currency Gap," United Press International, December 31, 2001 (*http://bit.ly/1j9onF6*).

communication among European countries, and between Europe and the rest of the world…. And open gateways and doors to symbolize the future—the idea of going through them to find a new currency."

The losing bills were either too dull or too fanciful, shot down with comments like "looks like Monopoly play money" or "it's too flashy and loud."[28] EMI found that the bill designs that seemed too playful (like the abstract entries by Robert Pfund, shown in Figure 1-17) were deemed untrustworthy, while more staid designs were "inconspicuous and cold." Despite the saying, humans do often judge books by their covers, and so in this case if the users don't like the way something looks, then they are less likely to interact with it.

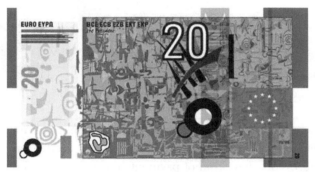

Figure 1-17. A rejected design for the Euro by abstract artist Robert Pfund, deemed too fanciful to be a commonly accepted currency

With cash, there is a cognitive association with how the money *feels* in your hand, as well as how it looks. Stick your hand in your pocket, and if you have any, feel the loose change rattling around in there. Over time, you have learned the ability to *instantly* recognize the texture, weight, and size of, say, a quarter versus a dime. Some countries have extended this variance in tactile form to paper money as well. Again, the Euro is a great example of fostering this kind of intimacy. Each denomination has a unique size, and is marked with numbers printed in relief and foil elements to signify their value (Figure 1-18). Tactile

---

28 "Euro Banknotes Test Results and Comments: Final Report," EOS Gallup Europe, December 6, 1996 (*http://bit.ly/1j9otwx*).

marks along the edges make it easy for the blind to recognize them by touch, and the relative sizes are a bonus for the rest of us, like merchants who need to quickly separate the 20s from the 50s.[29]

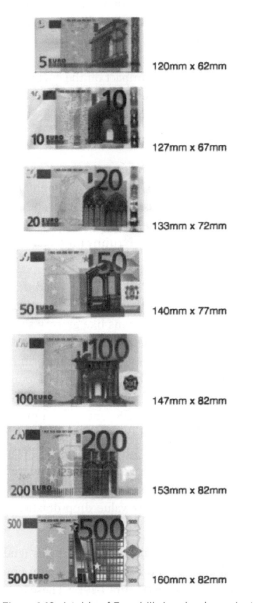

120mm x 62mm

127mm x 67mm

133mm x 72mm

140mm x 77mm

147mm x 82mm

153mm x 82mm

160mm x 82mm

Figure 1-18. A table of Euro bill sizes by denomination

29 "The Euro and the Blind," European Parliament, May 21, 2001 (*http://bit.ly/1oemoi9*).

Cultures around the world independently began to adopt the use of coins and bills as currency, in their own time, each with its own origins, materials, and denominations. The meaning of the symbols, typography, and material the currency is made out of are all contributing factors to a trustworthy aesthetic that is evident to both merchants and consumers. This is why drastic design revamps, such as the recent redesign of US $20s, $50s, and $100s, can lead to much public discourse, especially if it might have a negative impact on the currency's perceived worth. Let's explore two relatively recent real-world examples that illustrate this aspect of a currency's stability.

THE TROUBLE WITH SADDAM'S DINARS

Before the second Iraq War, Saddam Hussein decided to revamp all denominations of the Iraqi *dinar* to showcase his tyrannical might. For example, he ordered that busts of himself decorated with stately or military garb be added to each bill. Adding insult to injury, Saddam's bills were notorious for being poor-quality prints with runny inks, and were very easily faked.

Once Saddam's reign ended, the bills' accepted worth dropped drastically, which of course had dire effects on the local economy. Most Iraqis used only cash, and so everyday transactions like grocery shopping became extremely difficult, as most merchants refused to take Saddam's money...unless you happened to have an older dinar printed before Saddam's, which back in 1991 would have been worth around $3.25 in US dollars. After the second Gulf War and the ouster of Saddam, the value of 250 dinars dropped to 16 US cents, which meant that people had to carry *huge* wads of bills with them when they left the house. Imagine trying to pay for your gas or your phone bill with pennies or nickels, and you'll have an inkling of how inconvenient and worrisome this situation was for the typical Iraqi citizen. Imagine checking your bank account balance only to see its value drop drastically within the span of a few days!

In order to rectify this, in 2003 the occupying Coalition forces (and later the Iraqi Republic) worked to issue new banknotes based on pre-Saddam-era bills as an emergency measure (Figure 1-19).[30] These bills

---

30 "Iraq to Adopt New Currency," BBC News, July 7, 2003 (*http://news.bbc.co.uk/2/hi/ business/3052642.stm*).

replaced Saddam's face with symbols of national pride such as grana-
ries, date palms, and the Minaret of Samarra. This retro-revamp of the
dinar helped to stabilize the currency so that the cycles of daily commerce could start to recover (and of course it had the side benefit of
erasing the omen of Saddam's visage).

Figure 1-19. A dinar bill during Saddam's reign (top) and a post-war bill
(bottom)

BITCOIN FURTHER SHIFTS MONEY TO THE DIGITAL PLANE

Recently, new forms of completely digital currency have sprung to life
in online communities. Some are meant to be purely conceptual, staying within a digital realm, as with gaming (e.g., *Second Life* or *World of
Warcraft*). Others have made the leap to real-world markets, like Bitcoin
and Litecoin. The ultimate abstract currency, Bitcoin, was developed by

a faction of the tech community who were interested in creating a globally accepted digital alternative to centralized currencies. Purchases are made when Bitcoins are exchanged in public between peer accounts, with the intention that the community at large will self-govern and attest to the validity of transactions, all of which are listed in a public record (known as a *blockchain*). The intent was to create a pliant medium of currency that is free from both the bounds of the physical world and the whims of regulating institutions. In a practical way, it provides for simpler transfer of funds between parties, often anonymously. It makes situations like international wire transfers much easier, in that the user doesn't have to pay a transfer fee (upward of 10%) or exchange it for a relevant currency. Funds are available in seconds rather than two or three business days, which is great for merchants (though, as of yet, there are just a handful of online and brick-and-mortar stores that accept them; see Figure 1-20 for one example). Like the Euro, Bitcoin has an uphill battle to prove itself as a trustworthy payment medium.

Figure 1-20. Coupa Café in Palo Alto, California, accepts Bitcoin payments (courtesy of Kashmir Hill, Forbes)

Unfortunately, without an institution regulating a currency, human nature steps up to ruin potentially good things. An online store called the Sheep Marketplace experienced a massive heist in November 2013, resulting in the theft of the equivalent of $5 million in Bitcoins.[31] Someone was able to hack the market and sneak funds into a single Bitcoin account, while fooling other account holders into believing that their funds were still intact. This hack wasn't the fault of the Bitcoin network per se, but rather a weakness in the security of this particular web marketplace. Where bitcoins (and any other digital currency) are challenged in this case is that there are no government agencies like the FDIC that could reclaim and redistribute the users' compromised funds, as in the case of a robbery of a brick-and-mortar bank.

The financial world is currently abuzz with talk of Bitcoins, with respect to the disruption of payment systems. Each time Bitcoin pops up in the broadcast news cycle (in a good or bad light), there is usually a speculative rush that causes the value of one bitcoin to vacillate wildly. It jumped from $30 to $240 between March and April 2013, and ended the year at nearly $1,000.[32] As of this writing, Bitcoin is experiencing a relatively stable trend (hovering around $600–$650), but it is still considered a gamble as a widely circulated currency. These kinds of speculative bubbles (like the 2005 mortgage bust) are lucrative but troubling—especially when the potential of huge returns blinds those who join in the investment frenzy. This rapid fluctuation, coupled with the media's association of bitcoins with illicit black markets and money laundering means that their worth as a practical payment system is undermined...for now.

Summary

Over time, our money has mutated from precious, practical instruments of commerce to amorphous electronic data passing us by in the ether. The mechanisms we use to transact have evolved drastically, and will *continue* to evolve. Whether purchases are self-motivated or gifts for others, our financial instruments have become intensely personal—an extension of ourselves and our wants. We customize our

---

31 Adi Robertson, "Online black market members hunt down $100 million in Bitcoins, blame site owners for theft," *The Verge*, December 2, 2013 (*http://bit.ly/1oemy9f*).

32 Blockchain.info, January 2014 (*http://blockchain.info/charts/market-price*).

debit cards with pictures of kittens or our favorite sports teams. We fawn over elite status symbols like black or platinum credit cards. We collect rare coins and bills that tell stories of our country's history. We *touch* the cards and bills in our wallets every day.

Though money as an artifact means many things to many people, we all tend to gravitate to payment systems that are the most consistent, convenient, and relevant to the context in which we use them. Since most of us leave the house every day with a wallet or purse and a phone, two very *personal* items, it's only natural that these worlds begin to merge. How we use these new instruments will certainly be influenced by the emotional associations and mental models we have formed over thousands of years of transacting. We as designers should endeavor to keep in mind both the personal and historical context of money when creating new commerce experiences.

Further Reading

If you would like to learn more about the long and twisty path that payment systems have taken since the dawn of humanity, I highly recommend *The History of Money* by Jack Weatherford (Three Rivers Press). He excels at framing the advent of different payment artifacts from around the world with the reasons why these systems worked or didn't work for the culture that invented them. This book is a surprisingly easy read for such a complex topic.

For in-depth looks at the future of payments and banking, I strongly recommend seeking out the blogs of Dave Birch of Consult Hyperion, and Brett King, founder of Moven Bank and author of *Breaking Banks* (Wiley). Their irreverent takes on how mobile devices are changing the way we pay, bank, and identify ourselves are always insightful:

- Dave Birch (*http://www.chyp.com/media/blog/*)

- Brett King (*http://www.banking4tomorrow.com/blog*)

[2]

The Mobile Money Ecosystem

When a new startup sets out to build some revolutionary mobile payment app, the possibilities appear to be endless, prompting visions of happy users gliding through checkout lines with nothing but a wave of the phone and a jaunty tip of the hat. *No paper receipt for me, thank you!* Users will surely toss their plastic debit cards into a lake. *A paradigm shift!*

Yet the reality is that a mobile payment experience lives and breathes by the technological ecosystem that it is built upon. As with any digital experience, the ever dark and mysterious "backend system" can make or break your app, regardless of how usable and slick your UI might be or how many user personas you research and compose. If the cashier at the store can't see your customers check in on their point-of-sale (POS) app, or the register's near-field communication (NFC) reader doesn't "beep," then your users may be left red-faced and fumbling for that plastic card you've worked so hard to advance them away from.

End users could not possibly understand (or care) how payments technologies work behind the scenes; they expect only that this app will make their lives easier by expediting payments or helping them save money. They want to be assured that the app is maintaining their financial privacy and allowing them to keep track of their spending. Mobile apps in the financial space are rarely known for elegant interfaces, and this is often attributed to technical architecture challenges and lack of institutional agility. It is in your best interest as a product designer to understand the technology underlying *any* digital experience, so that you can anticipate any limitations or UX pain points that may occur. Unexpected latencies or loss in network connectivity to the phone, if not handled with appropriate messaging and alternate flows, can mar an otherwise gracefully designed app. In this chapter, we'll take a look at the most common technology approaches, with particular attention to the UX benefits and shortcomings of each (see Table 2-1).

TABLE 2-1. The three payment ecosystems in mobile commerce, with their user experience benefits and challenges

FRAMEWORK	BENEFITS	CHALLENGES	EXAMPLES
NFC	Transaction speed, secure storage of card data, no need for data network, can be wiped remotely	Complex ecosystem, lack of merchant acceptance in some markets	Isis, Google Wallet
Cloud	Works on most devices and OSes, variety of redemption methods (QR/barcode, geolocation)	Dependence on data networks, lack of security standards, higher processing costs for merchants means less acceptance	PayPal, LevelUp
Closed loop	Works on most devices and OSes, less risk for consumers, uses existing merchant POS accessories, often tied to rewards programs	Accepted only by sponsoring merchant; if linked to a debit/credit card as funding source, can be a security risk	Starbucks, Dunkin Donuts

Payment Framework Types

As Table 2-1 outlines, there are generally three types of payment frameworks that a mobile wallet or payment app may be built upon: NFC, cloud, or closed loop systems. The chosen route often depends on who is building it, and how she envisions her POS experience playing out. NFC is favored by issuers and mobile networks due to its high grade of security and risk management processes. Independent startups favor cloud-based wallets and usually go with linking their users' cards with a cloud-based service and using data connectivity, geolocation, or QR (quick response) codes/barcodes to transact. Merchants tend to choose closed loop systems so as to favor their own stored-value or reloadable gift card systems as the primary funding source.

These three ecosystems—NFC, cloud wallets, and closed loop—can even work together in the same wallet, enabling a versatile mobile wallet that is easier to distribute to different device platforms (for examples of the interplay of the three methods, please see Chapter 7). Each ecosystem may have its own benefits and drawbacks, so developers must weigh the cost of each approach and choose the one that would be best for them.

NFC PAYMENT APPS

NFC (Figure 2-1) is like many other wireless communication standards, such as Bluetooth or RFID (radio frequency identification), allowing two objects to exchange tiny packets of data. While Bluetooth or RFID can work when objects are several feet away from each other, NFC is more intimate—with a range usually around a centimeter. It can be used for all sorts of mobile use cases: sharing photos between friends, tapping a poster to get promotional media downloads, or reading a transit card to get the current balance.

Figure 2-1. Google Wallet is one example of NFC payments in the United States: once users link their cards to their Wallet account, they can tap their phone at any NFC-enabled point of sale (image courtesy of Google)

An NFC payment at the register typically relies on three key components: the NFC antenna of a mobile phone, a tamper-resistant secure element (a smart chip where the user's card data is protected according to EMV[1] standards) somewhere inside that phone,[2] and a contactless NFC reader accessory at the store's point of sale. A consumer with an NFC-enabled device can walk into any store that supports contactless payments and tap his phone on the reader to pay. To the merchant, it appears as if the user had swiped his card as usual (or entered a chip and PIN card, as customary outside the US).

NFC is now present in over 125 million mobile devices around the world.[3] It allows two devices (in this case, a phone and a POS reader), within an inch or so from each other, to exchange data. This electromagnetic conversation between the reader and the phone lasts half a second, during which time the POS reader retrieves data from the secure chip inside the phone. It's the same encrypted data that is written onto the magnetic stripe of your old plastic card, but with extra data and cryptograms added to the end of it that can have a lifecycle of validity.

The user experience of an NFC payment works like this: when the consumer approaches a payment terminal to check out, she opens up her app, enters a PIN, and, when she is ready to pay, taps a Pay button or just holds her phone over the reader. Alternately, she could just hold her phone over the POS reader without opening the app. These tapping interactions vary depending on the mobile contactless specification being used—that is, functional requirements dictated by Visa payWave, MasterCard PayPass, American Express ExpressPay, and Discover Zip—as well as how the issuing bank has mandated that its card product be presented at the point of sale. The POS reader alerts the consumer and the merchant with a loud beep, the consumer's phone vibrates or shows a confirmation message of some sort, and the transaction's done!

---

1   Acronym for Europay, MasterCard, and Visa; they wrote the specifications for how chip cards can be used.

2   Note that there is now the concept of tokenized locally hosted EMV card applets, which can be stored temporarily on the phone for NFC payments and periodically refreshed by the issuing bank. As of this writing, this method is available only on Android or BlackBerry devices thanks to host-card emulation. It is currently being tested by a handful of banks while awaiting certification by the payment networks (Visa, MasterCard, etc.). This method would eliminate reliance on mobile network operators for provisioning (getting the card onto the phone).

3   ABI Research, "Mobile and Mega Trends Report, Q2 2013" (*http://bit.ly/1oetkMe*).

In Figure 2-2 you can see an illustration of a typical mobile NFC transaction and the communication back and forth from the ecosystem, taken from a contactless reader patent for Verifone, a manufacturer of retail checkout systems.[4] At point A, the user has tapped the phone on the reader to complete a purchase at a bookstore. At point B, the reader shows that the purchase was successful, and the amount. Further data from the purchase (name of the merchant, time and date, anything you might see on a paper receipt) can be sent to the user's phone once the transaction travels through the traditional payment networks.

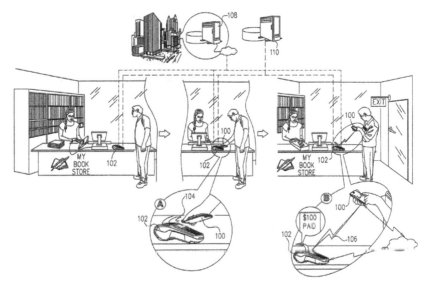

Figure 2-2. Illustration from a Verifone patent for a contactless reader for a point of sale

Although NFC (sometimes called *mobile contactless*) is well regulated and widely used in places like South Korea on public transit and vending machines, it has struggled to take off in other markets like the US and the UK.[5] This can be attributed to several factors, such as device

---

4 Verifone. Payment facilitating system for use with a mobile communicator utilizing a near field communication link. US Patent 20130030933, filed July 27, 2011, and issued January 31, 2013.

5 This could quickly change should Apple decide to incorporate NFC into the iPhone. That would mean significant changes to the phone's innards, so the jury is still out on whether this would ever happen. Find more about Apple in Chapter 7.

availability and merchant acceptance, but it is primarily due to the complex and fragmented NFC infrastructure that makes these types of transactions possible.

In Figure 2-3, you can see three parties working in concert to enable NFC payments on a phone. The essential players include the mobile network operator (MNO), a trusted service manager (TSM), and a service provider (could be a bank, merchant, or transit authority). In wallets like Isis, where multiple banks are involved, this ecosystem gets a bit more complex, with multiple TSMs and service providers.

MNO

Grants over-the-air access of its SIM card to the TSM so that it can install (and later remove) the bank customer's card data, which is usually contained in a small Java applet that only one wallet app can use.

TSM

Works on behalf of the bank to securely install and manage the card data on the device via the mobile data network.

Bank or issuer

Issues the card to the customer, and dictates how that card data can be used in the mobile context.

Service provider

Controls the user experience and facilitates communication between the bank, the MNO, and the customer. In some cases, the service provider and the bank are one and the same, as banks are beginning to incorporate NFC payments as part of their mobile banking apps.

In the last two years, there have been a handful of successful NFC pilots in various countries, prompted by collaborations between device manufacturers, banks, and telcos...and supported by the major payment networks such as Visa and MasterCard.

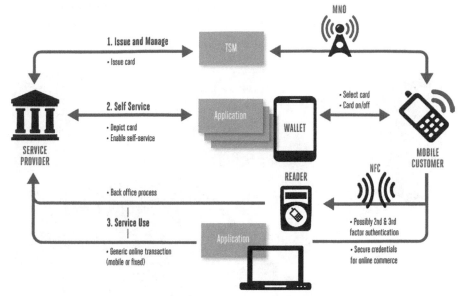

Figure 2-3. The components of the NFC ecosystem that make mobile payments possible (courtesy of the GSMA)[6]

At the London 2012 Olympics Village, only Visa cards or cash could be used to make a purchase, and every terminal was enabled for contactless payments. In all, 726 Visa staff, partners, Visa-sponsored athletes, and journalists were issued Samsung Galaxy SIII NFC phones equipped with a Visa payWave mobile app (Figure 2-4). They processed an average of 15 transactions each using their phones. After the event, Visa confirmed that 150,000 payments at games venues were made using the technology. That's 15% of all card payments, and most were at a value of £20 and under.

Here in the United States, U.S. Bank conducted two rounds of pilots (one in 2010 and 2013), providing pilot participants with iPhones equipped with a special case (between $20 and $50) that had an NFC antenna built in, plus a microSD to store their card data. Though the users enjoyed the speed of transactions and the futuristic "coolness" of tapping a phone to buy something, they balked at the unwieldy case accessory that was used in the pilot to power the iPhones with NFC.

6 Groupe Speciale Mobile Association, "The Role of the Trusted Service Manager in Commerce," December 2013 (*http://bit.ly/1oetuD7*).

Our phones are very personal objects, and it can be a real showstopper if any newfangled gadget negatively affects how we use them for other purposes, like decreased battery life or unwanted bulk.

Figure 2-4. Shoppers at the London 2012 Olympics could use an Android phone preloaded with a Visa payWave app to make purchases at stores in the Olympic Village

In Austin and Salt Lake City in late 2013, a consortium of US carriers called Isis operated an NFC pilot where users could tap phones to make payments and redeem local offers. Isis launched to the rest of the country in November 2013. Though initially mired by delayed release dates and an awkward user interface, Isis is certainly an unprecedented alignment between competing carriers in a concerted effort to advance the NFC ecosystem in the US. We'll take a closer look at the user experience of Google Wallet and Isis in Chapter 3.

Benefits

The primary benefit of the NFC ecosystem is consumer peace of mind, in terms of security. NFC payments are the most secure form of mobile transacting, requiring users to hold their phones very close to the reader in order to make a payment (see Figure 2-5). It uses powerful bank-grade security constructs, such as the smart chip on the device (which is nearly impossible for hackers to crack compared with apps that store the consumer's card data at the OS level or in a cloud service) plus secure over-the-air data connections, multifactor authentication,[7] and PIN codes to bar any malicious use of the app. If a user loses her phone, one call to the bank or the service provider sets the ecosystem in motion to either block a stolen phone from making unauthorized payments, or remove the payment functionality entirely.

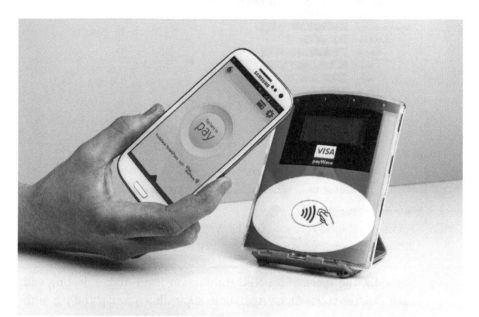

Figure 2-5. Tapping an NFC reader with the Vodafone SmartPass; in 2012, the Vodafone SmartPass pilot in Australia gave ANZ bank customers Galaxy SIII phones with an NFC wallet app preinstalled, to use at the 100,000 shops with contactless terminals in the country

Likewise, studies have shown that consumers are more likely to trust a mobile payment application if it is associated with their financial institution. In the chart shown in Figure 2-6, you can see that financial institutions like card networks and banks clearly win out over tech companies like Google or Apple and mobile network operators like Verizon or AT&T.

---

7 Multifactor authentication involves verifying something the user knows (a login and password) and something the user has (card details), and can even include fingerprint verification thanks to the iPhone 5S and some Android devices.

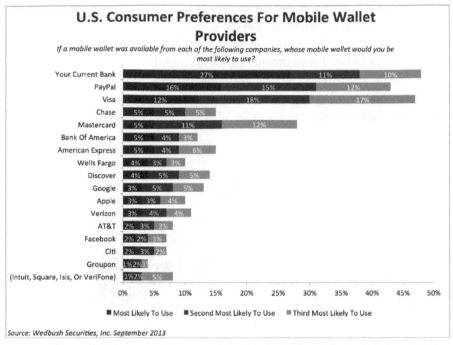

Source: Wedbush Securities, Inc. September 2013

Figure 2-6. A survey of consumers by Wedbush Securities in 2013 found that 27% would prefer mobile wallets sponsored by their bank

Secondly, the speed of an NFC transaction itself makes dealing with cash look resolutely Stone Age; some apps allow you tap and pay without opening the app at all (usually for low-value transactions or in-transit scenarios). The act of tapping an NFC device *feels* more natural to some users, as opposed to trying to properly align a barcode or a QR code to a scanner (which has to be an optical scanner, as the lasers of more common scanners will just bounce off the phone's glass screen). While it is true that adoption lags in the US compared with Canada and Brazil (which have higher penetration of NFC POS readers in retail), NFC can certainly be faster than credit cards and cash. An NFC transaction from start to finish is about a third faster than other forms of payment, as you can see in Table 2-2. The overall time it takes to pull out a leather wallet to remove a credit card, swipe it, type in a PIN, and collect a receipt from the cashier can be around 45 seconds, give or take (go ahead—time yourself!). An NFC payment, if you already have your phone out (which you probably did while you were bored and waiting in line) generally takes around 12 seconds. The additional second or two for the cashier to give you a receipt is also stripped away, as the app can now give you a fairly complete transaction record.

TABLE 2-2. Average transaction time according to payment method[8]

PAYMENT METHOD	TIME (SECONDS)
Checks	64
Credit/debit	48.5
PIN debit	44.4
Cash	28.5
NFC	12.5

Other benefits are the ability to pay even when there is no data network (like inside a big-box retail store where phone signals are diminished) because the system is built upon existing settlement and processing rails that we use every day with plastic cards. The system's interoperability with loyalty cards, transit ticketing, government identification, and building access/keyed entry makes it the primary contender for replacing all the uses of the old leather wallet.

Challenges

Critics of NFC question whether the technology will ever reach wide use, citing the lack of merchant acceptance, and that it doesn't truly save time at the register when compared with using a debit card or cash. Unfortunately, all the planets of the NFC ecosystem must align *before* the consumer can download the app and find a shop with a compatible reader. An initiative like Isis[9]—a rare joint venture of the three largest mobile carriers in the US (AT&T, Verizon, and T-Mobile) whose participants include card issuers like Wells Fargo and American Express—takes an immense amount of coordination and relationship building, which can be a lengthy investment of time. Countries like South Korea and Japan have had success with this system, because it

---

8 Nick Holland, "Contactless Payments and NFC in the United States: Beyond Science Fiction," Aite Group, LLC, January 30, 2008 (*http://bit.ly/1oetF1s*).

9 Note that in July 2014, the Isis consortium announced that it would rebrand to a new name, yet to be announced as of this writing. The intent was to avoid association with the militant group known as ISIS.

was generally lorded over by individual mobile networks or device manufacturers. Consortiums like these were a key element to getting this form of payment into the hands of consumers. The nuanced interplay of these parties has a noticeable influence on consumer experience, especially during the first use, when the user is setting up his phone for payments and downloading his card data.

For example, with some NFC apps, after the user downloads the app and registers, it may take anywhere from 30 seconds to 12 hours until the bank authorizes the TSM to install the user's card on the device. Designers would have to consider how to communicate to users that they must wait for a significant amount of time until their phones are ready to tap. Communication during the activation process must be transparent and reassuring, without overwhelming users with technical jargon. Any ambiguity during the onboarding process tends to make a bad first impression.

Another challenge is feedback in the form of information that can be shown to the user after the transaction is complete—essentially taking the place of a receipt. In some markets, the contactless readers at the register may not provide the app with complete transaction data when users tap their phones, such as the purchase amount or currency; they may send back only a vague "transaction data received" response, which can be somewhat confusing to consumers, causing them to rely on more traditional stimuli: a nod from the cashier and a beep from the POS to tell them the transaction was approved.

Merchant acceptance is always a challenge for mobile payment apps, and NFC is no exception (though it is the most widely accepted). The number of NFC-enabled points of sale varies from region to region. Places like Canada, France, Brazil, and Poland have contactless readers in every corner shop and taxi, whereas as of June 2013 there were only 500,000+ readers in the US. This number may grow within the next few years, thanks to the payment networks (Visa, MasterCard, American Express, etc.) adjusting their risk liability policies to place more responsibility on the merchants for fraudulent purchases, which would be reduced by EMV cards like the ones used for NFC. The burden will soon be on merchants to make sure their POS systems are upgraded with the latest accessories. But for now, just over 7% of the 7 million retail stores in the US accept NFC.

Another frustrating challenge to implementing an NFC payment app, and one that designers and developers typically have little to no influence over, is overall awareness. This does not apply just to potential users being aware of the service and its benefits (which is why we hire marketing folks). Consumer awareness is relatively easy to get a handle on, as more NFC-enabled devices are released into the market and users become more accustomed to using NFC to share pictures or check in at their favorite venues. A clear, strong marketing campaign combined with a successful user experience will help uneasy users feel more comfortable using their phones in this way.

But once the reader is up and running, a store may or may not have properly trained its staff in how it all works, prompting blank looks from the cashier if the customer has any trouble tapping her phone. Sometimes this kind of training is just not a priority, given how few NFC users are out there relative to people paying with cash or cards. More than a few times, I've pulled out my Google Wallet or Isis Wallet on my NFC-enabled Android phone at my local Whole Foods, only to find the employees had helpfully covered up their contactless reader pads with a placard plugging the weekly sales promotion or marketing (see Figure 2-7). Even if your favorite coffee shop does have a compatible reader, it must be correctly configured and in good working condition to accept a tap (from *any* contactless form factor, be it a phone or a card or a keyfob).

Figure 2-7. An NFC reader at Whole Foods, partially obscured by a placard

CLOUD

Storage "in the cloud" is a technology buzz phrase that has found its way into the payments world. Our documents and personal content are now readily available from any web-connected device, to use when and where we need them. Along these lines, in Chapter 1 we saw money become less tangible, and now thanks to mobile devices we can access our money from anywhere.

Considered by some to be the most efficient ecosystem, cloud-based payments require much less infrastructural heavy lifting than the NFC ecosystem does. A customer enrolls his card with a secure web service, and any payments made using a mobile device are charged back to that funding source. Sensitive card data is (hopefully) never stored on the phone. Instead, transactions are facilitated by the scanning of barcodes and QR codes in store (LevelUp), prepaying for a purchase from the consumer's device and picking it up (Square Order), or using geolocation to verify that an eligible consumer is present (PayPal Here).

The pioneer of this system as it began on the Web is PayPal, so it has the most users (15% of all mobile users as of this writing[10]), but scores of startups have now entered the fray. According to the Payments category on Angel List, there's around 1,100 and counting! In the case of the LevelUp app (shown in Figure 2-8), users present a tokenized QR code at a participating merchant, which then charges their linked funding source. The merchant simply scans the QR code with its proprietary LevelUp scanner, attached to a point of sale (LevelUp also has apps for merchants). The reader beeps, and a few seconds later, the user gets an electronic receipt. LevelUp also ties in rewards for frequent shoppers, so they can rack up discounts.

Rather than be tied to any single payment interaction, PayPal tries more of a "Swiss Army knife" approach in an effort to maximize the number of compatible merchants available to the user. PayPal incorporates as many payment methods as possible, including remote ordering, entering a phone number and PIN at the point of sale, using geolocation-triggered check-in, and even using Bluetooth Low Energy beacons (see Figure 2-9). The geolocation payment is especially forward-thinking.

---

10 Yankee Group report, "US Mobile Wallet Roundup: Gauging the Future Potential of Today's Solutions," February 27, 2014.

When a user is within several feet of a store, she can "check in," and her name and face pops up on the merchant's point-of-sale app. The customer only needs to say, "I'm paying with PayPal; I'm Lucy," and then she can grab her double latte and go.

Figure 2-8. LevelUp uses QR codes, which are linked to a credit or debit card stored in the cloud (image courtesy of LevelUp)

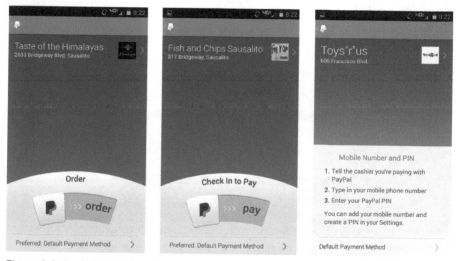

Figure 2-9. PayPal uses three different payment options (with more on the way), depending on the merchant's acceptance method: remote ordering (left), check in (middle), and through a phone number and PIN entered at the register (right)

Square is another proponent of cardless transactions via the cloud. The service was founded to rejuvenate the conventional POS and inventory system. It all started with using an elegant plastic card swiper that plugs into a phone's audio jack. The company recently retired one of its payment products, Square Wallet, a companion to its Register app where the user could link a credit or debit card, then simply check in to his favorite merchants and give his name at checkout, where his face and name would pop up on the merchant's Register app (Figure 2-10). It was a precursor to PayPal's geo-check-in payment feature. Shifting gears, Square launched a new product called Square Order (shown in Figure 2-11) that allows users to place orders at nearby restaurants with an elegant ordering process and one-tap checkout. All they have to do is walk or drive down to the merchant and pick up their order.

Figure 2-10. The Register app from Square, where customers could check in with their phones using the sister Wallet app (courtesy of Fast Company and Square)

Square and PayPal have oriented their products mostly toward making payment acceptance easier for merchants, by giving them lower processing fees and allowing them to take card payments with a card swiper accessory, and in the process upgrading the traditional "cash register"–style UI that plagues most point-of-sale systems. Ever watched a checkout cashier hunt and peck for that item you ordered? Companies like Intuit, LevelUp, and Revel are changing all of that, and passing the saved time to the store's customers. This paradigm is especially ideal for very small businesses, like those in the world of gourmet food trucks, where being able to accept all payment types on the go equals a boost in revenue.

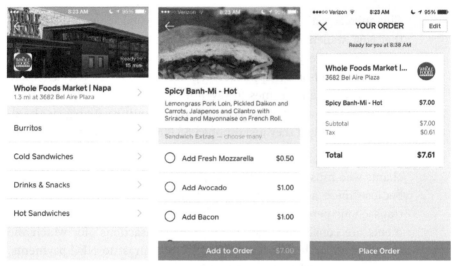

Figure 2-11. The Square Order app is an improvement over having to call in a to-go order—especially when you crave banh mi sandwiches at 8:30 in the morning like I do

Benefits

Cloud wallets are an agile alternative to the complex infrastructure of NFC, with much lower barriers to entry for both users and developers. A new startup looking to enter this space need only comply with card-holder privacy rules set by the Payment Card Industry Data Security Standard (PCI DSS), established by Visa, MasterCard, American Express, JCB, and Discover to provide multiple layers of protection for handling cardholder data and conducting digital transactions. After PCI compliance and the establishment of a settlement API to process payments, it's simply a matter of creating a user experience that will authenticate that the user: a) is who he says he is, b) has a valid card, and c) intends to initiate a payment. Registration for a new user is fairly pain-free (once he gets past the dreaded credit card form), and he can be up and running in less time than with NFC apps.

These kinds of apps are also hardware agnostic. There's no need for users to upgrade their devices to one that is NFC ready, for example, so this approach tends to work on all the major mobile platforms (unless it involves the use of Bluetooth Low Energy beacons, which require phones to meet the latest Bluetooth specifications).

Challenges

This approach still faces the same distribution and adoption challenges that NFC wallets do, in that both rely on the merchant having compatible hardware at the register—whether it's a laser scanner for barcodes, or a point-of-sale app that recognizes when registered customers are nearby. When it comes to revenue, merchants tend to stick with what works and aren't often prone to experimenting with register hardware—especially if they just dropped $5,000 on a point-of-sale system.

Another hit to cloud payments is that they're not as favorable to merchants who must work with an acquirer to process their transactions, because these acquirers typically charge higher processing fees for transactions perceived as being higher risk. Usually cloud-based payments are considered "card-not-present transactions" for which the store will incur higher fees.[11] This is in contrast to NFC payments, which act as "card-present transactions," meaning the cardholder *and* the card were present at the sale, so they carry a low settlement risk.

Cloud payment apps expose the user to the most security risk, once her card data has been transported and stored on the server. Though most apps like PayPal's allow the user to set a PIN or passcode to lock her app, the app is only as secure as the cloud server, the encryption strength of the app's communication, and the user's PIN selections. In a recent survey, nearly 9,000 iPhone users admitted that their screen lock code is 1234.[12] The second most popular lock code was 0000! Should a hacker eavesdrop on a user's mobile data traffic, using methods like Wi-Fi network spoofing—that is, setting up an innocuous-looking public Wi-Fi network called "attwifi-free" or "free public Wi-Fi"—then any phone that hops onto this network (either by user choice or because the

---

11 This is the purpose of the Card Verification Value, or CVV, also known as "the three-digit code from the back of your card." It confirms that a physical card was present at the time of payment.

12 Daniel Amitay, "Most Common iPhone Passcodes," Big Brother Camera Security, June 14, 2011 (*http://bit.ly/1oetJ1f*).

network resembles one the phone already trusts) provides a window for that hacker to see passwords and cardholder information being passed between the app and the cloud. That double latte might cost more than the user bargained for!

Another practical challenge here is that transactions aren't possible when the cellular network is unreliable or Wi-Fi is unavailable (see Figure 2-12). Even when data connectivity is not an issue, there is often a perceived latency while the user waits for confirmation of the transaction in the form of a push notification, SMS, or some other form of digital receipt. Even in today's world of lightning-fast 4G LTE networks and public Wi-Fi hotspots, just a short connectivity drop of a few bars is enough to slow or halt a cloud-based payment.

Figure 2-12. Cloud apps depend on data connectivity to facilitate payments in person; lapses in data connection often render them useless

CLOSED LOOP

Closed loop payment systems are like little jars inside a retail shop where the consumer can set aside her money for later use. They are based on stored-value cards that can be redeemed at only one merchant (like that $25 gift card for Best Buy your brother gave you for Christmas, and you forgot about it until Easter). A companion mobile app allows customers to redeem that stored value, usually by presenting a QR or barcode at the point of sale. Users can reload the card indefinitely, putting in only as much money as they intend to spend with that particular merchant, limiting the exposure of their financial details and bank accounts. This is also a great way for users to budget how much they spend on particular types of purchases, like groceries or restaurants. Merchants usually weave loyalty schemes and offers into their closed loop cards to keep their customers coming back.

The most successful examples of this system are the Starbucks and Dunkin Donuts apps (the latter is shown in Figure 2-13). Starbucks, notably, has processed 4 million payments a week since its app launched in 2011.[13] These apps also allow users to redeem loyalty points for free drinks, which keeps customers coming back in a caffeinated cycle of savings, and they are much easier than carrying around (and reloading) a clumsy plastic card. We'll take a long look at the Starbucks app as a case study in the next two chapters.

Benefits

Closed loop apps are inherently easy to implement from an acceptance perspective, as they are usually sponsored by the merchant itself. They are especially quick to release, thanks to the use of barcodes and QR codes, which can be read by most laser scanners already attached to modern points of sale (though it's unlikely that you'll find them at the corner grocery store). All the checkout cashier needs to do to accept the payment is to indicate that the customer is paying with a gift card.

---

13 "Starbucks Mobile Payment App Nears 4M Transactions Per Week," Mobile Payments Today, April 29, 2013 (*http://bit.ly/1oetUtb*).

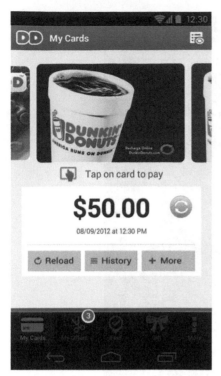

Figure 2-13. Dunkin Donuts lets users store and reload their gift cards in an app, which tracks purchase history and rewards (courtesy of Dunkin Donuts)

The user's risk can be very low, depending on how much money he loads onto the card. These low stakes make this system a good entry point for users who want to try out mobile payments for the first time. As these cards are often tied to rewards programs, the user can also be shown a points tracker, which encourages him to earn enough points to get free items and save money on future purchases. Because it's on a mobile device, a closed loop app that can track the balance of a store's card is a huge improvement over the plastic version; the user won't have to ask the merchant to swipe the card to look up the balance, or be surprised when the balance is lower than he expected. These apps are entirely device agnostic, and can be deployed on any mobile device...or even smartwatches (Figure 2-14)! They can be used even when there isn't a data signal—a leg up on cloud-based payments.

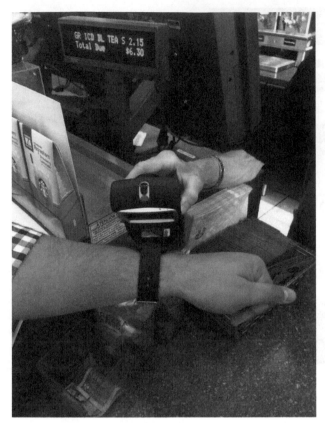

Figure 2-14. The author, paying with a Pebble smartwatch, linked to a Starbucks app

Challenges

These experiences do need wireless connectivity to an extent, so that the user can see her current balance *before* she attempts to scan it at the register (lest she incur angry stares from her fellow shoppers for slowing down the checkout line). Otherwise, she is going into the purchase without knowing if she has enough funds.

Closed loops systems are just that, closed: they can be used only at one associated retailer. This clutters the user's mobile home screen with icons of her favorite shops, as opposed to offering her "one wallet to pay them all." There are gift card wallets, like Gyft and GoWallet, that can store cards from multiple merchants, but they won't include rewards points and may not have balance tracking.

A minor UX challenge here is the brightness of the user's screen and ambient light reflection. Barcode scanners can be fickle creatures, needing just the right light conditions and laser alignment for a good read. Starbucks has utilized the mobile OS to reduce scanning issues by overriding the device's brightness setting so that the screen shines at the brightest level when the barcode is displayed.

QR codes are not standardized, so they're vulnerable to malicious redirection or copying by scammers. 1D barcodes are standardized but are limited to 10–20 characters, which doesn't allow them to store much data, like randomized tokens. They are both easily duplicated. If the user leaves her phone unattended while the code is displaying, someone could (in theory) grab the phone, take a screenshot, and email it to himself.

Summary

Each of these systems has its own benefits and drawbacks, and so a payments developer—whether a financial institution, mobile carrier, or startup—must choose the system that is most appropriate. Though businesses often make decisions like this by weighing revenue models, time to market, or customer ownership, in the end it is ease of use, security, and added value that drive consumer adoption.

In the next chapter, we'll take a close look at the user experience of mobile wallets and payment apps that utilize NFC, cloud, and closed loop systems to see how these underlying technologies play out when they are implemented.

[3]

Leading US Mobile Payment Experiences

Today there are mobile payment initiatives by everyone from traditional financial networks like Visa and MasterCard to upstarts like Loop and Clinkle looking to cash in on the gold rush for consumer mind-share of the mobile payments space. Figure 3-1 illustrates what the US mobile payments field looks like to date, with startups like LevelUp giving established financial institutions and technology companies like Google and MNOs (Isis) a run for their money.

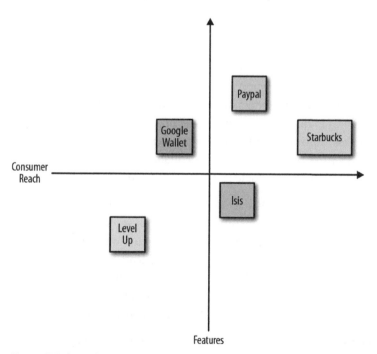

Figure 3-1. Apps from startups like LevelUp are butting heads with larger wallet efforts like Google Wallet and Isis in terms of consumer adoption and feature offerings

As we saw in Chapter 2, there are three primary ecosystems that power mobile commerce: NFC, cloud, and closed loop payments. The structure and performance of these distinct ecosystems have a significant impact on the mobile consumer's experience at the point of sale. In this chapter, we'll closely examine some leading experiences in the US mobile brick-and-mortar payments market, highlighting the innovations and shortcomings of their designs. In particular, we'll focus on three key aspects of payments design that I feel are the most crucial to the success of a mobile payment experience:

Payments
Using the app at a point of sale

Feedback
Instructing the user before and after transactions

Security
Protecting the user's financial privacy

NFC

GOOGLE WALLET

The first NFC-based wallet widely available in the US, Google Wallet made brave first steps into the world of mobile transacting in September 2011. The Wallet team aligned with key players in financial and mobile networks to set NFC payments in motion. First Data provided TSM services, while Citibank was the first to issue prepaid MasterCards enabled with PayPass. Sprint provided access to secure elements on a select range of Android phones, starting by collaborating with Samsung to produce one of the first Google flagship phones, the Nexus S.

Early adopters of Google Wallet encountered a clean, friendly UI (indicative of the design paradigm shift at Google that would soon permeate all of its products). The launch was supplemented with strong online, print, and in-store campaigns that helped educate users about using NFC for payments and finding participating merchants. Each Wallet came with a $10 prepaid card, which users could reload by linking a credit card if they weren't Citibank MasterCard customers.

Users could enroll their rewards cards from merchants like American Eagle, Office Max, and Macy's. Google Offers was also seamlessly integrated, including a collection of NFC-only discounts at stores like Gap and Banana Republic as an added incentive to start using the Wallet. The current iteration of the Wallet is a thinner, more focused experience: all payments are processed by way of a digital card profile temporarily stored on the phone via host-card emulation (as opposed to being on the SIM, like Isis). Offers are now redeemed by barcode.

Overall design

Strengths:

- Google products' latest design philosophy is in full effect here, with a clean, card-based UI (see Figure 3-2), clear calls to action, and Android OS best practices at work.

- Google Wallet 2.0 features a slide-out navigation menu for key features like cards, money transfers, loyalty programs, and local offers.

- Friendly tone and labels guide the user through payment experiences.

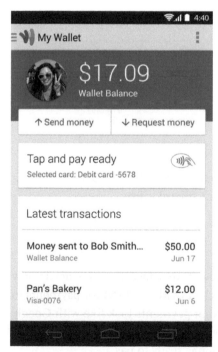

Figure 3-2. Google Wallet's refreshed design (courtesy of Google)

- Users who are reluctant to add a credit or debit card to their phone can opt instead to preload their Google Wallet Balance (Figure 3-3), which can be used at the time of purchase, similar to a prepaid card.

Figure 3-3. Users can opt to use either a credit or debit card for purchases, or load money onto their Wallet Balance as the funding source of a transaction, online or in store

Weaknesses:

- Card images are generic, and do not reflect the actual card that was registered (i.e., a Wells Fargo or Citibank card).

Payments
Strengths:

- The app-launch-to-payment flow is very fast; the user needs only to have the app open and unlocked (with his PIN) for payments to take place (Figure 3-4 shows what payments look like with Google Wallet). The first few times you use the app, there's a helpful message that tells you when your app is ready to pay.

- There is an audio cue and short vibration when the phone comes into contact with the reader.

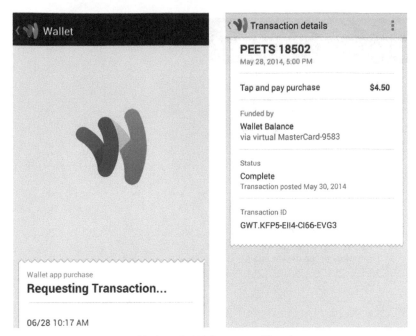

Figure 3-4. A payment with Google Wallet at a coffee shop

Weaknesses:

- There isn't always an indicator that the card is turned "on" and ready to pay. Users may not understand that when the app is open and their phone's NFC antenna is on, their payment card is considered "armed and ready."

- Except during the onboarding process, no instruction is given to the user regarding *how* to pay—that is, how to hold the phone over the reader or what to look for in a store that accepts NFC (only when reader is tapped *without* opening the app do you see an instructional diagram with tips on how it works).

Feedback

Strengths:

- When something goes wrong, Google Wallet displays helpful instructions, telling the user to try the tap again or check with the cashier for confirmation (Figure 3-5).

Figure 3-5. A helpful error message, directing the user to check with the cashier to confirm the transaction; this might appear if the reader was not compatible, or if the NFC handshake encountered a conflict

- If the NFC antenna of the phone is turned off, or another NFC wallet is in use,[1] Google Wallet informs the user as soon as she opens the app rather than waiting until she attempts to pay (Figure 3-6). The error messages also give the user a button to tap that will bring her to the screen in her device's Settings menu where she can quickly rectify the issue.

Weaknesses:

- Transaction feedback (refer back to Figure 3-4, center) is vague: "Requesting transaction…" feels like the app is asking *permission* to make a payment, when in fact the payment has already happened. Something less robotic-sounding, like simply "Paying now…" or "Payment completing…" would be more effective.

---

1 This tends to happen with Android phones running OS 4.4 or above, where HCE (host card emulation) allows for multiple NFC wallets on one phone. The phone's NFC controller can use only one wallet at a time, and the user can usually set one wallet as the "default."

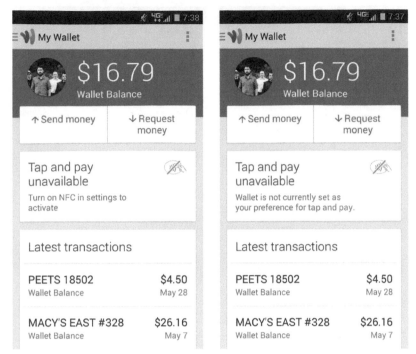

Figure 3-6. Two cases where the user might encounter problems paying with her phone: the NFC antenna is off (left), or another wallet is occupying the NFC function (right)

- Even on "smarter" readers that can return rich transaction data (amount, currency, merchant name, address) the Transaction History in the app may not reflect this information right away. More information about the purchase may not display until the payment is processed and reported back via the Wallet's cloud services (which requires data network access).

Security

Strengths:

- The user is greeted with his account identifier (Gmail address) when the app starts up (Figure 3-7, left), which is a nice touch of personalization that says, "this app remembers me."

- The passcode lockout feature activates after 15 minutes or 1 day of user inactivity. The passcode is also used to "lock" the app to prevent fraud, and allow for authorization of larger purchases—say, over $150.

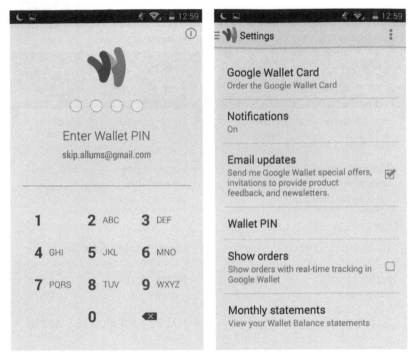

Figure 3-7. Google Wallet's PIN screen and security features

- Progressive numeric fields are used as opposed to one long field, allowing for quick passcode entry, in four taps (similar to a phone lock screen). The app uses a custom keypad, rather than the stock OS one, which prevents eavesdropping by any malicious apps that may be installed somewhere on the device (Figure 3-7, left).

- The user (or thief) has six attempts to get the passcode correct. Exceeding this limit locks the app and blocks any card data present in the OS memory to be invalidated by the cloud service.

Weaknesses:

- The wallet passcode is labeled as a "PIN," so debit card users might be tempted to reuse their ATM PIN, which is risky. A safer label might be *mPIN* or *passcode*.

- There's no indication of help if the user forgets his passcode until he enters an incorrect one, at which point a "Forgot PIN?" link displays.

ISIS

Isis is the other significant NFC wallet in the US, and is a joint venture between the three major carriers: Verizon, AT&T, and T-Mobile. Because Isis is managed by network carriers, customers' card information is usually stored in a secure element installed on their SIM card. The service first trialed in Austin and Salt Lake City, and launched to a wider audience in the fall of 2013. Isis reports having up to 20,000 activations per day as of April 2014, and now is often preloaded by the carriers on supported Android phones.[2]

Like Google Wallet, Isis navigated some rough waters at the outset in terms of merchant/carrier alignment and hasty redesigns, resulting in a series of launch dates being pushed back. Now the service is poised to gain significant adoption in the US market, given its availability on the big three carriers. Isis has made preemptive strikes to address the key challenges of the mobile wallet experience: adoption and value-added services, like offers and loyalty cards. In the two cities where the app was piloted (Salt Lake City and Austin), Isis took on the cost of upgrading many local merchants' POS systems to support NFC payments. This allowed more merchants to accept it, leading to around 10 transactions a week from Isis wallet users.[3] Isis also incorporated an NFC offer and loyalty card system from participating merchants, which could be redeemed at the register with one tap (i.e., payment plus an offer, payment plus loyalty point, etc.).

Isis was also able to bring more card issuers on board, allowing for customers of Chase, American Express, and Wells Fargo to download their cards to the wallet.

Overall design

Strengths:

- Helpful instructions are displayed during the onboarding process (Figure 3-8), guiding the user through setup and payments.

---

2 Michael Abbott, "Averaged 20,000 New Isis Wallets Per Day Over the Last Month; Growth Rate Doubled Over Prior Month; Preloaded on 14 Devices with More Coming," May 14, 2014 (*http://bit.ly/1oewyiH*).

3 Dan Balaban, "Isis Gears Up for National Launch Despite Challenges Ahead," NFC Times, May 23, 2013 (*http://bit.ly/1oewIXg*).

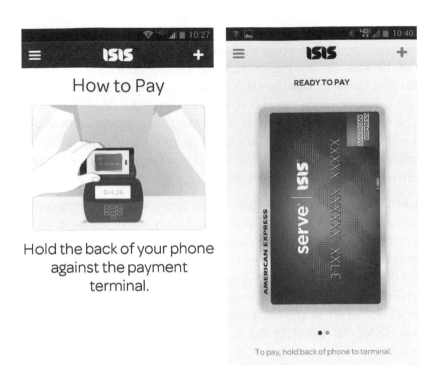

Figure 3-8. Isis has clear instructions throughout the app, often using diagrams to explain how to use different features

- The app includes familiar navigation patterns, and has a contemporary look and feel.

- Like Google Wallet, Isis comes with a prepaid card from American Express Serve, so the user doesn't have to add her bank cards to the app if she's hesitant due to security concerns.

- Users are rewarded with cash back for purchases made with the app, and given discounts from a handful of large brands that have partnered with Isis (e.g., Jamba Juice, Foot Locker, Toys R Us, and Coca Cola).

- Users can also add a few loyalty cards to the app, which automatically count any purchases made to the merchant's loyalty system or points aggregator.

- A map search is included for nearby participating merchants.

Weaknesses:

- There is no customization of cards or card nicknames.

- There is no transaction history to show the user a log of payment activity, acting as a digital receipt.

- The onboarding process is somewhat fragmented, with web-based enrollment of cards, rather than enrollment being handled within the app (Figure 3-9). When the user taps the Add Card button, she's taken to the phone's web browser to fill out her card issuer's enrollment form. This was likely to accommodate the disparate authentication requirements for the three card issuers. It's a subtle difference, but a significant one—users may view jumping around between parallel apps to be too much trouble, and this design opens up the probability of navigation issues or service errors. More importantly, it may discourage users who are wary of logging into their bank's web services using their phone.

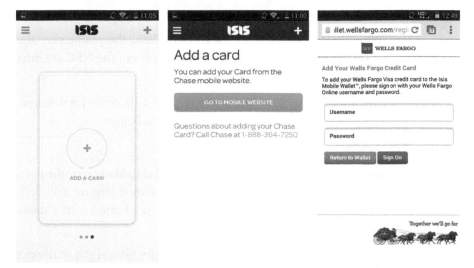

Figure 3-9. To add a card to the app, the user is redirected to the phone's web browser to log in with her online banking credentials, rather than being able to add the card within the experience

Payments

Strengths:

- The Ready to Pay indicator (Figure 3-10, left) shows when a card is ready to pay.

Figure 3-10. Paying with an American Express prepaid Serve card

- Subtle instructions tell the user how to hold the phone over the reader, by placing the back of the phone (where the NFC antenna is) over the reader at the register.

- The card slides up when the reader (Figure 3-10, center) is detected, giving a clear indication that a payment has begun.

Weaknesses

- When an Offer (e.g., $5 off at Jamba Juice) is turned on by the user, there is not much indication on the Pay screen (Figure 3-10, left) of which offer is turned on. The only clue is a button with a vague label, Clear Offers.

- Likewise, when the payment is done (Figure 3-10, right), it doesn't tell the user which offer was applied to the purchase. He has to rely on the cashier or the paper receipt for this confirmation.

Feedback

Strengths:

- The animation, sounds, and vibration paired with messaging is general enough to show that a payment has been *attempted*, without any conflicting messaging from the point-of-sale reader (for instance, if the card was declined, or did not complete for some other reason).

- The confirmation screen clearly shows which card was used for the transaction (Figure 3-11).

Figure 3-11. The somewhat vague confirmation screen showing the user that a transaction has taken place

- Flipping a card image over reveals basic details about each card in the wallet, such as the last four or five digits of the card, and the type of card it is. The back of the Serve prepaid card is especially helpful. It shows the last known balance, so the user knows how much she can spend, and has links to add more money or use the cards for bill payments online.

- If the user opens the app when her phone's NFC antenna is switched off, an alert pops up to inform her and show her where to turn it back on (Figure 3-12).

Figure 3-12. An alert that the NFC antenna is off

Weaknesses

- The display of transaction details is fairly vague (Figure 3-11). For example, it doesn't display the amount of the purchase, the name of the merchant, which offer was redeemed, or which loyalty card was used. The screen doesn't seem definitive.

- The user must still rely on the cashier or the POS to tell her whether the payment was successful.

Security

Strengths:

- The PIN screen uses a large, custom numeric keypad, instead of using the stock OS keypad (see Figure 3-13, left).

- The user can lock his app using his PIN at any time—a Lock Wallet button is readily available from the slide-out menu (see Figure 3-13, right).

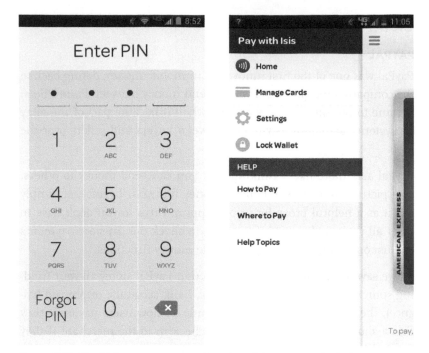

Figure 3-13. The PIN screen prevents fraud, and the user can lock the app at any time from the app's menu

- As with most NFC wallets, the user's card data is stored inside the device on the SIM card, in an encrypted container

- The user's name, email address, or full card numbers are never stored or displayed in the UI, which reduces exposure of financial data.

Weaknesses:

- As with Google Wallet, the passcode is labeled as a PIN (which may put cardholders at risk if they use their debit card PIN).

- The letters on the keypad aren't really necessary, as most users opt for numeric passcodes, especially when they are meant to be four digits or characters.

Cloud Wallets

PAYPAL

PayPal was one of the first innovators in mobile money, dating back to the company's inception as a way to send money between Palm Pilots. It came to prominence in payments when it became part of the eBay ecosystem, facilitating payments between buyers and sellers over the Web.

PayPal acts more like a banking app: you can send money to others, take pictures of checks to deposit money into your balance, or simply use it as a helpful proxy for web shopping carts so you don't have to enter all your credit card information to check out. In-store payments are just one feature in a suite of mobile money functions.

As we saw in the previous chapter, though PayPal stores all your funding sources in the cloud (linked cards, bank accounts, or prepaid balance), the app is agnostic when it comes to how users pay once they find a shop that uses it. They might check in to the merchant if they are within range, and the merchant sees the user pop up on its own PayPal POS app. The user might place an order for pickup from the app. PayPal has also partnered with large retailers like Home Depot and Dollar General to let users enter their mobile phone and PIN at the register—no phone required. It doesn't stop there. PayPal is usually on the cusp of any new technology that could aid in faster and safer mobile transactions, including using Bluetooth Low Energy beacons to check users into a store, scanning QR codes on a bill at a restaurant, and employing fingerprint scanning technology to unlock the app or authorize purchases.

Overall design
Strengths:

- Users can link several cards and bank accounts to the app, or preload their Wallet Balance. This gives them more options to check out with.

- Because PayPal uses various payment methods, the list of accepting merchants is greater than that for most cloud-based wallets (see Figure 3-14 for an example of two payment options, and a list of merchants).

Figure 3-14. PayPal acts as a wallet, allowing the user to link several accounts, and supports several payment interaction types

- Users can browse nearby merchants without having to log in first.

- The app is available for Apple, Android, and Windows devices.

Weaknesses:

- The app depends on data connectivity in order for the user to be able to log in, pay, place an order, or really do anything other than browse for nearby merchants.

Payments

Strengths:

- The app shows the user a comprehensive list of all the nearby merchants, which can be browsed in map or list views (Figure 3-15). The distance and the address of each shop are easy to find.

- Icons and buttons clue users in as to which kind of payment they take: a clock or button for pre-paying for something they'll come in to pick up later or have delivered, a phone for merchants who will see users check in and charge their PayPal account for the order, and no icon for larger chains that accept just a phone number and PIN at checkout (Figure 3-16).

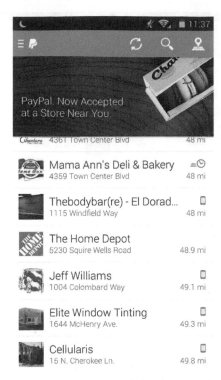

Figure 3-15. Shop search for the PayPal app

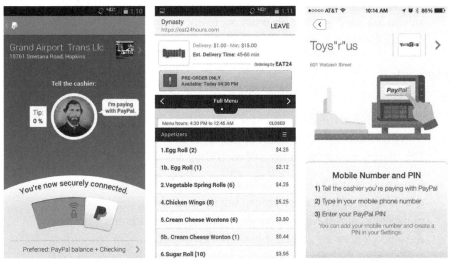

Figure 3-16. Depending on what the store supports, users may have very different payment interactions: geo-check-in (left), remote ordering (center), and entering a phone number and PIN at check out (right)

- For check-in payments, users can add a picture of themselves to their profile, so that the merchant will recognize them.

Weaknesses:

- Experiences are fragmented. Though it is convenient that so many merchants accept PayPal, the three different checkout flows are so drastically different that the user isn't quite sure what to expect from each transaction (Figure 3-16).

- For remote ordering, PayPal may pass the user off to a third-party site, like EAT24, to complete the transaction.

- Remote ordering and check-in payments require a data connection.

Feedback

Strengths:

- The user is kept informed with helpful error messaging written in plain English, without any technical jargon.

- Users are provided a transaction history with a robust record of recent payments (Figure 3-17). Wallet balances are clearly displayed.

Figure 3-17. The account view on the Windows app shows clear available balances for the user's prepaid account, as well as recent transactions

Weaknesses:

- A data connection is required, so a digital receipt is not immediate and may be delayed if the connection is slow.

- The user is still fairly reliant on the store cashier to verbally confirm whether the payment was successful.

Security

Strengths:

- The full details of the user's linked cards and bank accounts are never displayed on screen (just the last four card or account numbers).

- Most activities like transfers and payments or changing account settings can be accessed only in password-protected areas of the app.

- Users can lock the app with either their PayPal email and password, or their phone number and PIN (Figure 3-18). This lets them enter the app with the security credential they feel most comfortable with (or can remember at the time).

Weaknesses:

- Sensitive user data, such as home addresses and expiration dates, is displayed for some stored cards. These are completely unnecessary to show in the app. If this information is cached in the OS memory, it can be exposed.

- Complex passwords (mix of letters, symbols, and numbers) are not required.

- The PIN fields in the app use the OS keyboard (Figure 3-18), which could expose users' PINs to any malicious apps that may be running in parallel on the device.

Figure 3-18. PayPal lets users choose how they want to log in: through their email and password or with their phone number and PIN

LEVELUP

Founded by Boston-based mobile gaming shop SCVNGR, LevelUp payments are centered on the use of QR codes to transact, while tying in loyalty points and offers for a growing number of participating merchants. LevelUp boasts a user base of a million people and close partnerships with small businesses and financial institutions. LevelUp links its QR code payments to the user's credit or debit card, which is stored outside the LevelUp servers by payment processor Braintree. Merchants use a phone or tablet with the LevelUp POS app, and can scan customers' QR codes with their own device's camera or a proprietary scanner accessory. LevelUp is exploring the use of code scanner/NFC reader combinations, which suggests a more agnostic approach to conducting transactions on a mobile device.

Overall design

Strengths:

- LevelUp maintains a cheerful and consistent design across several platforms (iPhone, Android, and Windows Phone).

- The design is simple, with no frills. There are no overwhelming menus or processes, and onboarding (which starts from the screen shown in Figure 3-19) is fairly quick and pain free.

Figure 3-19. LevelUp uses QR codes for payments at small businesses

- The merchant directory search results (Figure 3-20, right) are displayed in a logical manner, calling out enticing offers.

Payments

Strengths:

- The app is ready to present to the reader as soon as it opens (Figure 3-20, left); no additional taps or loading times are needed.

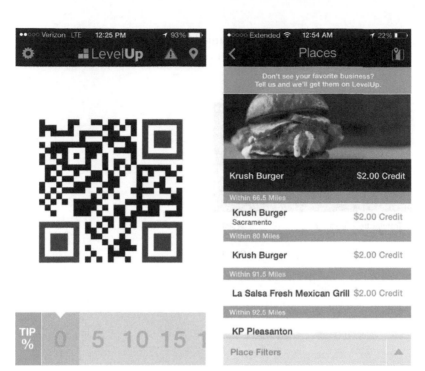

Figure 3-20. Payments are efficient, thanks to a ready-to-scan QR code and a helpful merchant directory that shows nearby shops and the rewards they offer

- Users can add a tip to their bill using the tip slider at the bottom of the screen, which changes the QR code accordingly.

- The QR code itself is large, so it's easy for merchants to scan.

Weaknesses:

- A data connection is required for the user to get a digital receipt in the form of an SMS or push notification.

- It can only be used at merchants that also have the LevelUp POS app.

Feedback

Strengths:

- Within a minute or so after the merchant accepts payment, the user can view an itemized receipt.

- The receipt is usually accompanied by a visualization showing how much more the user needs to spend at a particular shop to earn cash back (Figure 3-21).

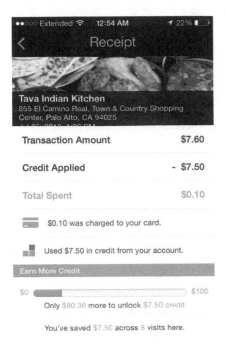

Figure 3-21. Itemized digital receipts and reward tracker visualizations

Weaknesses:

- A data connection is required, so the receipt takes some time to display and may be delayed if the connection is slow.

- The transaction history is oddly buried under Settings; it could be more prominent in the navigation.

Security

Strengths:

- LevelUp lets the user set an optional four-digit passcode or PIN to lock the app (Figure 3-22).

- The app uses a custom keypad, rather than using the stock OS keypad.

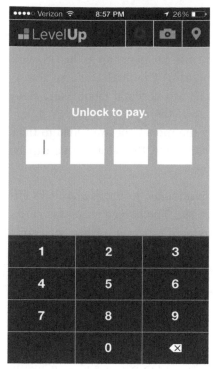

Figure 3-22. An optional passcode lock keeps users' QR codes from being accessed without their permission

> Detailed information about credit or debit cards is never shown in the app, and in fact the user's card information is stored by payment gateway Braintree. The app relies on a tokenization system instead to process payments via the QR codes, which are randomly generated for each user.

Weaknesses:

- There's no clear way for users who have forgotten their passcode to reset it or receive a reminder, unless they block the app after five incorrect attempts.

Closed Loop

STARBUCKS

Starbucks is the most widely used mobile payment app in the US, with 10 million active users as of March 2014.[4] The Starbucks app acts as a "gateway drug" for consumers who are hesitant about using their phones to pay for goods and services. If their phone is lost or stolen, consumers are only at risk of losing the money they've added to their reloadable Starbucks card. Credit cards and PayPal accounts can be linked to the app for autoreloads as well.

The app stores the barcode and card number of the user's Starbucks gift cards, which can be reloaded as needed. The barista scans the card's barcode to process payment. The payment experience is part of a suite of features like a store locator, rewards tracker, and gift card ordering. Starbucks is also integrated with Apple's Passbook, which aggregates gift card and ticketing features from a variety of iOS apps.

Overall design

Strengths:

- Rather than using a more traditional tab bar or slide-out menu, the app has a dashboard (Figure 3-23, left) that gives the user fast access to payments, as well as spending history and a store locator.

- The app encourages repeat visits with free drink rewards by showing graphs and animations to indicate the user's progress to the next reward milestone.

Payments

Strengths:

- Payments with the Starbucks app are very simple: present the barcode of the user's registered Starbucks card to a barcode scanner attached to the point of sale.

- Users may also redeem drink rewards using the same barcode.

---

4 "Starbucks Mobile Payment App Nears 4M Transactions Per Week," Mobile Payments Today, March 12, 2014 (*http://onforb.es/1wRlyfV*).

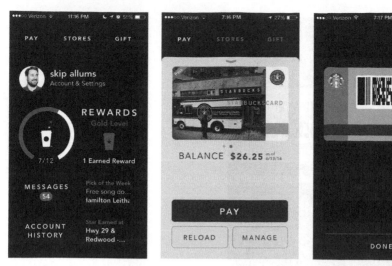

Figure 3-23. The Starbucks app was recently redesigned, with new features and emphasis on earning rewards

- Screen brightness is automatically adjusted to the brightest setting for easier scanning.

- A shortcut feature called "Shake to Pay" (Figure 3-24) lets users pull up their Starbucks card to pay from any point in the experience.

- Payments can still be processed even if there is no data connectivity.

Weaknesses:

- The dashboard is heavily weighted to rewards and marketing messages.

- The button for Pay is at the top left of the screen, which makes it difficult to reach during one-handed use.

Feedback

Strengths:

- Shortly after the purchase, the user is shown a receipt, which displays the store information, time, and date, along with the amount and which card was used (Figure 3-25, left).

- The tip feature lets users choose from preset amounts to add after the payment has already been made.

Figure 3-24. The Shake to Pay feature provides a shortcut to the payment screen

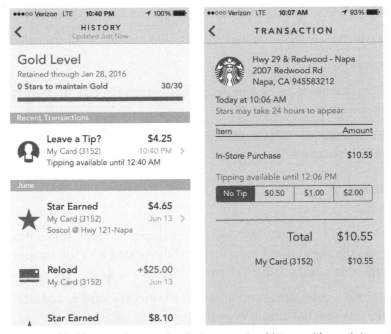

Figure 3-25. The app shows a detailed transaction history with receipts, and lets the user add a tip to the transaction after the fact

- After the user hits the Done button on the pay screen, the app checks the card's balance and updates it. The balance is also checked anytime the app is opened, so the user can always see the latest balance.

Weaknesses:

- The user must still rely on the cashier to confirm whether the card has scanned correctly.

- The app never shows a confirmation of payment during the interaction, unless the user actively goes back to the Dashboard and taps on Account History.

- An itemized receipt is sometimes delayed, though the user eventually receives a push notification with an updated balance.

- It may take a few minutes for the card balance to update within the app, if the data connection is slow.

Security
Strengths:

- Even though the financial risk to consumers is low, Starbucks still allows them to lock the app with a four-digit passcode (Figure 3-26).

- The app uses the term *passcode* instead of *PIN* and follows best practices for numeric passcode patterns.

- The passcode is "offline," so no data connection is needed to access the app.

Weaknesses:

- Because the app uses a barcode, a thief could just as easily take a screenshot of your barcode if the phone is left unattended, and use that at checkout.

Figure 3-26. Starbucks uses the label "passcode" for the lock screen, insead of "PIN"

GOWALLET

GoWallet is an app built by the Blackhawk Network, which provides payment card technology services to major financial institutions and retailers. GoWallet offers a mobile version of its impressive catalog of aggregated retailer gift cards. You have probably seen its gift card mall kiosks and end caps in large grocery or retail chains.

Remember that stack of gift cards that you got for Christmas from distant relatives? The cards will probably sit in the back of your junk drawer, until you find them months later when digging around for a flashlight. Around $1 billion in gift cards goes unused every year, often because we forget to put them in our wallet or purse before we head out to shop.[5] With GoWallet, consumers can import their gift cards

---

5 Quentin Fottrell, "$1 Billion in Gift Cards Go Unredeemed in 2013," MarketWatch.com, December 2, 2013 (*http://on.mktw.net/1oewYWg*).

(say, from Safeway, Burger King, or Home Depot) into the app, and use them at the register by displaying a barcode. This helpful feature does away with the need to carry around that $20 Applebee's gift card "just in case"; now it's right there in your phone! GoWallet also has a large catalog for purchasing digital gift cards from its product line, which you can then send to your friends.

Overall design

Strengths:

- GoWallet uses familiar navigation patterns that follow the relevant platform (e.g., iOS, Android) guidelines.

- Gift cards are presented in an easy-to-use list view (Figure 3-27, left), which resembles slots in a physical wallet.

- The app is complemented by features like balance tracking and reloading for each card.

- The app can store several cards from any supported retailer, so it reduces the number of plastic gift cards the user must carry around.

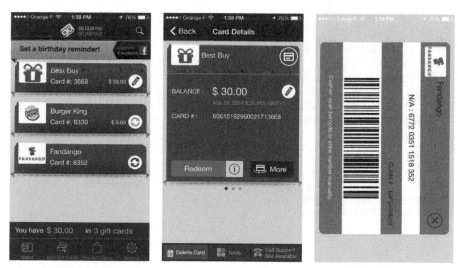

Figure 3-27. GoWallet stores gift cards, so the user doesn't have to carry around the plastic ones

Weaknesses:

- Many UI elements have no visual touch feedback, leaving the app feeling somewhat flat and unresponsive.

- There are several buttons with mysterious icons that require excessive pop ups and dialogs to explain their function. In Figure 3-28, for example, the dollar sign icon means "real-time balances may not be available," and the card icon means "please keep your original plastic card."

Payments

Strengths:

- Tapping the Redeem button on a GoWallet card displays a large barcode in landscape view, which makes for easy scanning at the register (Figure 3-28).

- If the barcode can't be read by the scanner, a numeric redemption code is also clearly displayed, so that the merchant can read it if necessary.

Figure 3-28. Barcodes are shown in landscape view for easier scanning

Weaknesses:

- There is often an excessive lag (a loading dialog) between the time the user taps the Redeem button and the barcode displays, which slows down the checkout experience.

Feedback

Weaknesses:

- GoWallet can't really tell the user *when* a payment has happened or for how much. He has to rely on POS for confirmation.

- The card's balance does not update after the user closes the bar-code screen after a payment. He must tap the Refresh button to get a new balance update. It's best to avoid extra steps like these.

- Some cards don't have balance checks at all, so users are directed to track it "manually" or to call a service number to check the balance (Figure 3-29).

Figure 3-29. Balance checks are not supported for every brand in the GoWallet catalog, so users may or may not be able to find out how much is on their card as they spend it, unless the cashier scans it for them

Security

Strengths:

- GoWallet allows the user to set a PIN for protecting her stored gift cards (Figure 3-30).

Figure 3-30. The GoWallet PIN screen

Weaknesses:

- The app allows several incorrect entries, which opens it up to brute-force PIN hacking.

- GoWallet uses a native keypad, which opens it up to malicious pattern-recognition attacks (especially on rooted Android devices).

- There's no clear way for the user to reset her PIN if she has forgotten it.

Summary

Though all of the apps covered in this chapter are essentially doing one thing—enabling users to make purchases using their phones—the user experience of each has subtle differences. Regardless of the technology these apps are built upon (the cloud, NFC, etc.), the more successful experiences have solid payment flows and clear feedback at the point of sale. Personal privacy is top of mind for most mobile payment users, so payment apps must also have some kind of locking or failsafe mechanisms to prevent theft or misuse. Less successful interactions are those that are ambiguous, leaving users unsure of what has transpired once they're checking out.

[4]

Building Trust into Mobile Payments

One of the key tenets of human/computer interaction is to avoid inciting anxiety in the user, which can be caused by uncertainty about negative events.[1] This is especially true when dealing with people's hard-earned money. Eliminating that uncertainty with design is a matter of addressing or finding out what your users expect from an experience, and catering to those expectations as much as possible, using common user interfaces that the user will recognize. With nascent technology like mobile payments, there are less abundant examples of successful design patterns than, say, for ecommerce shopping carts or browsing a social network feed. Still, there are some emerging patterns and best practices that we can look to as good (or bad) examples.

Don't Design for Early Adopters, Design for Everyone Else

Mobile payments are not really a new thing. Consumers in places like Japan and South Korea have enjoyed immensely popular mobile payment initiatives since 2004, beginning with services like FeliCa and NTT DoCoMo's *osaifu keitai* ("wallet phone"), with transaction volume surpassing ¥1 trillion by 2007.[2] They have also been using the same phones as door keys and airline boarding passes. So now that all these technologies exist in the mobile space, how come we aren't using them every day here in North America?

---

1 Phoebe C. Ellsworth, "Some Reasons to Expect Universal Antecedents of Emotions," in *The Nature of Emotion: Fundamental Questions*, ed. Paul Ekman and Richard J. Davidson (New York: Oxford University Press, 1994), 152.

2 Masaki Yoshikawa, "Mobile Wallet Service in Japan," NTT DOCOMO, Inc., October 31, 2008 (*http://bit.ly/1xNIOoG*).

The easy answers to the adoption question are generally centered on the fact that swiping a plastic card still works (mostly) and chicken-and-egg scenarios: mobile payments are built upon an outdated financial infrastructure,[3] or merchants won't adopt new point-of-sale technology, or telcos like those in the Isis collective have placed a chokehold on the mobile ecosystem. These are, of course, valid challenges, but I see a much broader, more difficult challenge: consumers are not yet *entirely* comfortable with the idea of using their phones to pay for things.

There are many points in the mobile payments supply chain that present technical challenges to adoption, such as compatible phones (in the case of NFC) and point-of-sale upgrades (like QR code scanners and NFC readers). NFC in particular requires business relationships between the bank and the mobile network operator, which are not always harmonious. Once the user has the right phone, then gets his card on his phone or links it to his app account, there's no guarantee that his favorite merchants will even be able to accept a mobile payment. All this makes it hard for a user to start using his phone to transact, even if he were *totally* on board with the idea of his phone having access to his bank account in some way. Institutions in the related verticals (financial services, telecommunications, retail operations) don't typically work together, unless they see a compelling consumer demand for a new payment method. The reason why NFC has become popular in places like South Korea is thanks to close collaboration between these disparate parties to bring new technology to the consumer. In the US, there are signs of joint ventures at this scale, like Isis (the three major MNOs) and MCX (retail brands), which are starting to inch the bar forward in terms of commercial visibility. In the end, I don't think it matters if the impetus of a payments revolution begins with a startup or with a respected financial brand, but what is clear is that industry-wide initiatives to improve payments technology would be a large contributor to mobile payments becoming more widespread.

Even if the stars of the mobile payment ecosystem align, there is still one key element that is less tangible but can make or break a mobile wallet, regardless of the method it uses (cloud, NFC, barcodes, etc.).

---

3 Jose Pagliery, "95% of Bank ATMs Face End of Security Support," CNN Money, March 4, 2014 (*http://cnnmon.ie/1xNJanO*). Did you know that 95% of ATMs in the US run on Windows XP? Scary!

That element is the consumer's trust in the experience, and it is the largest hurdle that mobile wallet designers and developers must tackle in order to build a successful payment system.

Of course, all new inventions must overcome the growing pains of gaining consumer mindshare, just as using the Web to shop, date, and rent vacation homes was slow to be adopted widely when those options came to market. If someone had told me five years ago that banks would be banging down my company's door to get mobile check deposit (i.e., account holders take pictures of their checks and deposit them digitally) built into their banking apps, I would have questioned that person's sanity. One great example of this is when University Federal Credit Union, the largest financial institution in Austin, Texas, first launched mobile deposit capture in its banking app. Within the first eight months, its members used their phones to deposit $16 million in checks.[4] These days, most major banks have this feature, with very similar usage figures. It's in our nature as humans to be skeptical of new technology, but this skepticism is not impervious. We are, of course, capable of change, if it's to adopt something that is convenient and reliable and that improves our daily lives in a profound way. Over time as we try new gadgets or ways of doing things, we begin to trust them—if they *work the way we expect* and don't provide cause for grief. Consider how often you do any of the following now, versus 10 years ago:

- Write a check
- Balance a paper checkbook
- Print out an online map for driving directions
- Visit your local bank branch
- Use a pay phone

My favorite quote on our capacity to adopt new ways of doing things, when it comes to the financial world, comes from Susan Crawford, Harvard Law professor and past advisor to President Obama on technology and innovation policy:[5]

---

4 Mobile Deposit Case Study, Mitek Systems, 2012 (*http://bit.ly/1xNJp2g*).

5 Aaron Smith, Janna Quitney Anderson, and Lee Rainie, "The Future of Money," Pew Research Center, April 17, 2012 (*http://bit.ly/1xNJCTd*).

There is nothing more imaginary than a monetary system. The idea that we solemnly hand around printed slips of paper in exchange for food and water shows just how trusting and fond of patterned behavior we human beings are. So why not take the next step? Of course we'll move to even more abstract representations of value.

The sea change inherent in mobile payments will not happen overnight. These new interactions face an entirely unique and complex adoption challenge because these apps intend to revolutionize a common task that we all do several times a day: purchasing something or paying someone. One criticism of mobile payments (often directed at NFC, but it applies to any mobile payment method) is that it's a solution looking for a problem. This point rings true—as of today, most consumers are just fine with swiping a plastic card. The current system works consistently, even if it's running on decades-old technology. It's generally reliable, as long as the magnetic stripe on the user's card hasn't worn out, and the store's card readers are functioning properly. No one could argue that there is a pretty low learning curve to using cash or cards. If consumers do eventually switch to paying with a phone, their mental model will remain rooted in the stimuli of the brick-and-mortar checkout experience: wait in line, be greeted by the cashier, open a leather wallet, swipe a card, type a PIN, hear the register beep, take the receipt, pick up the bags, etc.

What's even more daunting is that we are talking about *combining* two very personal objects: our mobile devices and our money. We never leave home without them—though I think that our phones might be dearer to us (a Stanford student survey in 2010 found that 69% would be more likely to leave their wallet at home than their iPhone[6]). Both of these hold significant places in our lives, and compromising either is something most of us would like to avoid at all costs. Likewise, consumers are understandably concerned with their financial privacy in this new paradigm. Since you are reading this book, you probably feel (as I do) that mobile devices and money go together like chocolate and peanut butter, but it's important to keep in mind that not everyone feels this way. Before the user taps that Register button on a welcome screen, she needs to be assured that the provider of the mobile experience will

---

6   Lance Whitney, "Stanford Undergrads: iPhones Are Addictive," CNET, March 10, 2010 (*http://cnet.co/1xNJSSa*).

protect her money, and that she will not be exposed to fraud or information privacy breaches. Once that faith is broken, it's nearly impossible to earn it again.

It is rather ironic that mobile payments are so untrusted by the general public, when traditional payment methods like cards and checks are in fact much less secure, and easily compromised or faked. Sure, a user's credit card has a magnetic stripe or an encrypted gold chip that locks down the account number and payment data, but what happens when someone steals his wallet? When was the last time a sales cashier asked to see the back of your card to verify that your signature matched? Are you one of the 12.6 million consumers who has had their identity stolen and used for unauthorized purchases?[7] Consumers are now more wary of their financial privacy than ever before: the Unisys Security Index in May 2014 found that 59% of Americans were extremely worried about hackers obtaining their card details. Financial fraud was their greatest concern, even greater than terrorism (47%), epidemics (34%), or going broke (30%).[8]

Consumers have good reason to be worried. Even large retail brands struggle with the assurance of security, as Target saw in December 2013 after its registers were hacked and cardholder information was compromised. The Heartbleed attack of OpenSSL in early 2014 compromised the passwords of many high-traffic websites (Facebook, Google, Amazon Web Services). These high-profile security breaches only contribute to the fear that hackers are out there, chiseling away at the walls that keep consumer information from falling into the wrong hands.

So mobile commerce has an uphill battle to fight. Of the mobile wallet usability testing sessions I have observed or moderated, an overwhelming dichotomy emerged, no matter how many users were able to complete the test's payment tasks successfully, or how nice they thought the animations looked. Users generally fell into one of two camps:

---

7 "2013 Identity Fraud Report: Data Breaches Becoming a Treasure Trove for Fraudsters," Javelin Strategy and Research, 2013 (*http://bit.ly/1xNK97H*).

8 "Unisys Security Index: US," Lieberman Research Group, May 13, 2014 (*http://bit.ly/1xNKpnh*).

Early adopters

Love the futuristic sexiness of buying stuff with their phone. Had previous experience using the Starbucks app, PayPal, or Square.

Everyone else

Felt anywhere from "mildly apprehensive" to "scared shitless" at the thought that their credit card number is stored inside a technological black box that they have never heard of, and don't understand.

There are, of course, nuanced subgroups in both of these, but the second group, "everyone else," is the one we as designers need to reassure, particularly as we build onboarding and payment interactions. Ideally, our efforts should go a few steps beyond finding the most "trustworthy" shades of blue, or sprinkling arbitrary "lock" icons everywhere.

Consumers' concerns are multifaceted, and fall into these four trust categories:

- The security of their bank account information
- Use of personally identifiable information
- Control of when and how payments can be made
- Contingencies for theft or loss of their device

Designs that successfully address these four areas will imbue a holistic impression of trustworthiness in the app experience. Falling short on any of these aspects will trigger doubts in the user's mind.

A recent report published by the Federal Reserve Bank of Boston reflects the four trust categories, chief among them being the exposure of their identity, and the fear of what might happen if their phone goes missing (Figure 4-1).

Let's look at those first three responses to the survey, as they're fairly interrelated. It's clear that the surveyed consumers were most concerned with identity theft. It's truly frightening to think that a thief could eavesdrop on or steal your phone, then learn everything about you: your name, your address, your relationships, your pictures, your credit card numbers, and more. This is why designers should take care never to display on screen any information that would personally identify the user.

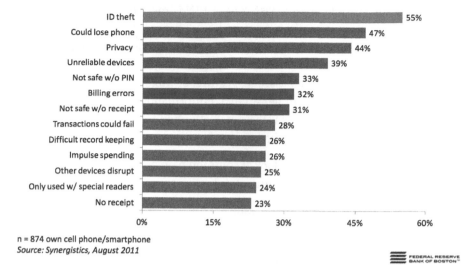

n = 874 own cell phone/smartphone
Source: Synergistics, August 2011

FEDERAL RESERVE
BANK OF BOSTON™

Figure 4-1. Consumer concerns related to using mobile devices for payment
(courtesy of the Federal Reserve Bank of Boston)[9]

The next concern for users was the loss of their device, which would
trigger the first concern—identity theft—as well as the inconvenience
of having to cancel any cards that might have been linked in some way
to their phone. The third one, privacy, is a bit vague. Privacy could be
the personal sense: who they are, where they live, or their phone number. In the financial sense, privacy could refer to their account numbers, balances, and spending history. These are typical of the grave concerns that run through a user's mind when he first encounters a new
payment app, either by seeing a friend using it or noticing it in his app
store.

Financial privacy rights are heavily protected by global regulators (like
the PCI Security Standards Council), especially around what we in the
financial service industry call *cardholder data*: the cardholder's name,
card numbers, expiration dates, PINs, and customer verification codes
(the three digits on the back of the card or four digits from the front of
the card, in the case of American Express). Industry security standards
dictate that the most effective preventative measure against those three
scenarios taking place is the use of a consumer authentication factor.

---

9   Elisa Tavilla, "Opportunities and Challenges in Broad Acceptance of Mobile Payments in
    the United States," Federal Reserve Bank of Boston, July 24, 2012, 17 (*http://bit.ly/
    1xNKDuI*).

Asking a user to enter a password or PIN is more often a welcome task than an annoyance. Even if a user doesn't have an NFC wallet or PayPal on her phone, she is now likely more accustomed to using complex passwords (a mix of letters, numbers, and symbols) as well as locking her phone with a passcode, gesture, or fingerprint. She will expect any app that deals with her financial information to have similar affordances. You can never pay too much attention to the areas of an experience where users might have cause for alarm.

Now, we will take a hard look at common pain points where mobile payment users feel the most uncertainty:

- Onboarding and registration

- Security options

- On-screen display of sensitive data

- Getting help

These four interaction families are where users are most likely to second-guess a financial app, especially if they encounter something unexpected. These complementary use cases are what I like to call the *bookends* of the payment experience (users signing up for the service, setting up their payment preferences, and finding help when they have questions), so it's important to make them as seamless as possible. These use cases will most likely come into play before the user even gets to the checkout line.

Onboarding and Registration

A user's first encounter with your app is a do-or-die moment. If at any point the user is not sure what your app does or feels overwhelmed by the registration process, he will instantly question the overall security of the experience and drop out. An effortless onboarding process is essential for any application, but this is especially true of a mobile financial experience. Relying on the consumer's familiarity with the brand is not enough. He must be assured that the app he's downloaded is clear about its purpose and will protect his financial privacy.

THE FIRST SCREEN

Users opening your app for the first time may expect to see a walkthrough, login forms, your logo, and maybe some slick animations. Even if their first task is to sign up or log in, don't skip out on the opportunity to state exactly what the app *does*. Never take for granted that the user has read through all the features in the app store listing. You could accomplish this with a simple statement like "MobilePay lets you pay [securely] for things with your phone!" You could also explain your app's purpose with a brief animation, or over two or three screens that state the benefits and features of using the app. Avoid wordy explanations, or long demo videos—just cut to the chase!

Calls to action like "Log In" or "Sign Up" should, of course, be obvious to the user, but don't force her to go through a registration process without first walking her through the app's key features.

Both LevelUp and Dash (Figure 4-2) use the start screen as an opportunity to communicate clearly what the app's primary features are. The Sign Up and Log In buttons are prominent, offering distinct paths for new users who want to sign up, and returning users who want to log in. Compare these with Google Wallet (Figure 4-3), which tells me zilch about what the app does or what will happen when I sign in with my Google account. The goal here is to be absolutely clear what the benefit will be to users, so they can decide whether or not it's worth their time.

Figure 4-2. LevelUp and Dash's start screens

Figure 4-3. While I appreciate that Google Wallet saves customers the step of entering their Gmail address, it doesn't say what the app does—what exactly are they signing up for?

WALKTHROUGHS AND DEMOS

Usability best practices would stipulate that if your application needs a tutorial, then maybe it's too complex. As designers, we've had it instilled in us to avoid over-embellishing. Keep it simple, Stupid...right? Mobile payment apps can be an exception to this rule, as most users aren't accustomed to using their phones to pay for things. They will probably need a little bit of instruction. Even if they are familiar with the general concept, your particular app's payment interaction may have subtle nuances (as we saw in the previous chapter) that make it different from one they have used before. For example, a customer who is familiar with using the Starbucks barcode for payment may not be familiar with the NFC tap-to-pay method, at least for the first few uses. You should include a brief introduction to demonstrate how paying works, or to point out navigation elements that will likely be used the most. There are two optimal moments in which a tutorial like this can be placed: on the start screen before the user signs up, or following registration.

If you decide to place a walkthrough before enrollment, strive to cover the general app functionality and its benefits, and limit it to three or four screens. Content placed before enrollment should follow a concise format, almost like an elevator pitch: what the app does, why users should use it, how it works. Use visual elements like diagrams and animations in concert with text to get the concepts across. Ideally, a Close or Get Started button should be plainly visible, so users don't have to swipe through the whole walkthrough or watch the complete animation if they don't want to.

Before the user registers, both Isis Mobile Wallet and PayPal (Figure 4-4) use animations to show how a typical payment works, so there are no surprises when the user gets to the register. Be sure to make your tutorials available from secondary Help or How To menus, so that customers can view it again later, as LevelUp has done in a section called How It Works (Figure 4-5).

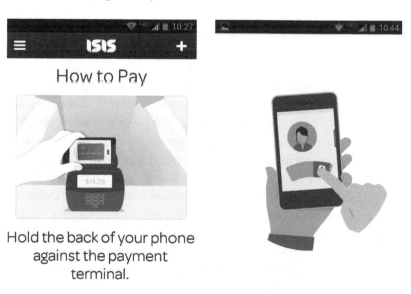

Figure 4-4. Animations can demonstrate payments during the onboarding process: from left, Isis and PayPal

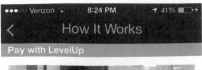

Figure 4-5. LevelUp provides a step-by-step guide that can be recalled at any time

Walkthroughs don't have to be limited to marketing bullets and instructional animations. Take the time to call out your security model as a feature, like any other selling point. You don't have to use detailed schematics or process flows to show how user data is encrypted as it moves over the payment network. A general statement or diagram is enough to assure users that yes, you are being careful with their financial privacy. The bPay trial (Figure 4-6) from Barclay's Bank Delaware did a great job of addressing this common onboarding concern: on the screen that explains the part of enrollment where users must link a card to the service, there is a simple statement below the graphic that clarifies that their card data is never stored on the device. Don't assume that users know the difference between local memory storage and storage on a secure hosted service, or that they'll know where their personal data will be kept. Don't be vague, either—your users aren't stupid. Compare bPay's onboarding with Kuapay's (Figure 4-7), which touches on the topic of data security, but in kind of flimsy way: a giant lock on a phone image (which tells the user nothing, really). There is a vague statement promising that the app's security "surprises even the security experts." That *sounds* impressive, but there's not much to reassure the user here.

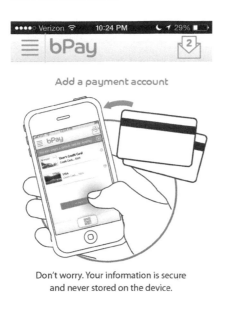

Figure 4-6. An onboarding screen from bPay (by Barclays Bank Delaware) that addresses how users' financial information is secured when they add cards to the service

Once your users have completed their enrollment, you can provide them with a tour of key features to help orient them. This can be focused on areas like how to start a payment, where to find the settings menu, or how to navigate to other areas of the app. This kind of tutorial works best at the home screen as a transparent overlay. You may also consider walking users through a payment demo, so that they will know what to expect when they make their first payment. Users should be able to dismiss the tour overlay with a tap or swipe, but let them bring it up again from a Help or About menu, in case they need a refresher.

More Secure Than Plastic
Our patented security model surprises even
the security experts. Pay with confidence
when you use Kuapay.

Figure 4-7. Kuapay could be clearer about its security framework in this walkthrough; it is best to explain this important concept in terms that are general enough for most users to understand, while being as accurate as possible

LevelUp (Figure 4-8) employs helpful pop-ups or toasts to call out key features of the app upon first use, but some of them are vague. *Who is supposed to scan the code?* The customer? The merchant? A more accurate description would be "Show this code at the register to pay."

Figure 4-8. LevelUp uses pop-up hints or coach marks for new users'
Registration

PayPal (Figure 4-9) shows an overlay upon first use, explaining its custom iconography and directing the user to the slide-out nav for more features. This is especially helpful if there are key icons that may not fit into the standard pantheon of mobile iconography. These initial walkthroughs and how-to's are a thoughtful way to ease users into using their phone as a payment instrument. Whether used as a welcoming experience or as an interstitial while the user account is being set up, these visualizations can alleviate users' anxiety about getting to the register and not being sure what to do. After all, no one wants to be the schmuck holding up the line!

Figure 4-9. PayPal employs an overlay to direct the user to frequently used UI elements

Registering and enrollment is the most challenging pain point for financial apps. Legalese, awkward button labels, and endless, *endless* forms all present points of friction that can cause a user to give up and delete an app. Though the flow of signing up a new user varies greatly depending on the payment method and required security constructs, there are a few best practices that can make onboarding quick and painless.

Reducing the number of "required" data fields is the easiest way to reduce the amount of effort inherent in a registration flow. One common road hazard is the dreaded credit card form. Partnering with banks is the only way of circumventing this step, as users could link their source cards and accounts via an existing banking credential or token, like their online banking login. Otherwise, you could expedite the process of adding a card by using a character recognition API for credit cards, like card.io, or simply by limiting the required fields to the bare minimum, namely:

- Card number

- Expiration date

- Customer verification code/security code

- Name as it appears on the card

- Billing street address

- Zip code

City and state can generally be drawn from the zip code, so they aren't *necessary*. There is also no need for the user to select the type of card (Visa, MasterCard, Discover, etc.), as the format of the card numbers can tell you that, thanks to standards set by International Organization for Standardization and the International Electrotechnical Commission.[10] From the first six digits of the card number (called the *bank or issuer identification number*), you can deduce the card type as well as the bank that issued the card (see Table 4-1). That's potentially four data points that the user won't have to enter manually!

TABLE 4-1. Examples of the four major card number types

American Express	Starts with 37XX XXXXXX XXXXX
Discover	Starts with 6011 XXXX XXXX XXXX
MasterCard	Starts with 51XX XXXX XXXX XXXX or 55XX XXXX XXXX XXXX
Visa	Starts with 4XXX XXXX XXXX XXXX

Cover and Venmo (Figure 4-10) capture card details in a simple form that fits in the top half of the screen. Fields like card type and city/state are bypassed in favor of dynamic field validation and OCR capture with the phone's camera. Compare this with the Dunkin Donuts app, which has a much longer form, with a total of 12 data entry fields. Even worse, the form does not obfuscate card details once they are entered, which could make users feel that their financial data is exposed. Of course, you will want users to have the visual feedback of seeing which numbers they've entered, but once the card number field is no longer active, I recommend hiding all but the last four digits of the card. Registration

---

10 ISO/IEC 7812-1:2006, "Identification Cards -- Identification of Issuers -- Part 1: Numbering System" (*http://bit.ly/1xNKWFy*).

should not exceed three or four steps or screens. Throughout the process, users should be given an obvious indication of how many steps are required, and where they are in the flow as they progress. In the mobile context, this can be shown as a progress bar, or simply with text in a prominent location, like "Step 2 of 4." This is comforting to users, in that they know approximately how long it will take to set up their account, and it gives them a fair idea of how much information they may need to volunteer.

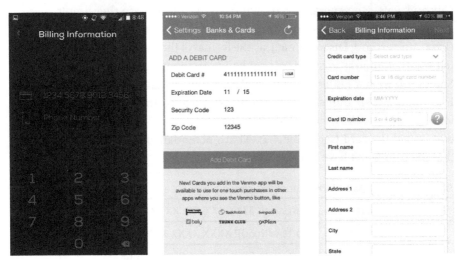

Figure 4-10. Adding a card with a form should be as efficient as possible, as Cover (left) and Venmo (center) have done; avoid unnecessary data entry, as seen in the Dunkin Donuts app (right)

Uber (Figure 4-11) shows users a progress indicator that turns green as users complete each step in the process. Venmo uses text along the top bar to tell users how many steps they have left to go. Both apps take care to explain to the user *why* they are asking for certain types of personally identifiable information.

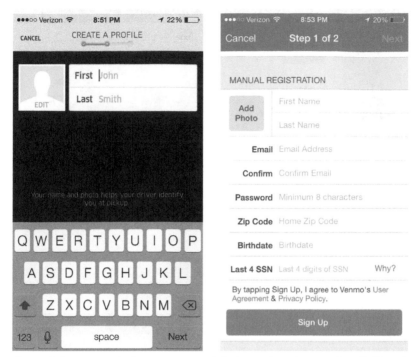

Figure 4-11. Progress indicators are used during registration for Uber (left) and Venmo (right)

Likewise, if there is a point (usually at the end of the registration process) where users must wait while some behind-the-scenes process carries out (like activation of the secure element in NFC payment apps), you should inform them how long the process will take, and concisely explain why the delay is necessary. Ideally, we want to avoid this scenario, but if this process is absolutely necessary, it should be made apparent to the user that all is well. For example, Google Wallet (Figure 4-12) displays friendly, concise messaging to let users know that their phone is being set up for payments, explaining what is being done in the background (the phone is securely receiving contactless card data), and wraps up with a cheerful success screen once the process is complete. If possible, avoid blank screens with stock loader animations, and, as an alternative to the usual "Loading...please wait" messaging, utilize this interstitial period to guide the user through other areas of the app that *don't* rely on the background process, like merchant locator maps or settings.

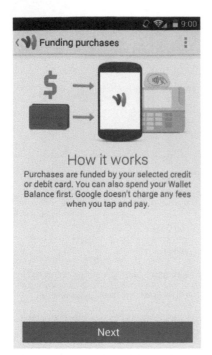
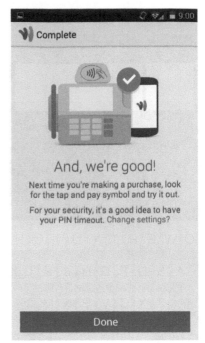

Figure 4-12. Google Wallet, in the process of setting up the user's phone for NFC payments

The frustrating paradox about terms and conditions in applications is essentially: *no one reads 'em, but you can't get rid of 'em.* Most likely you will be required to show these at some point to users, and they should have ready access to them at any point in the experience where it might be appropriate, such as in a supplementary About menu. Still, for those who *do* like to read the fine print, try to incorporate legal disclaimers and service statements in a way that is not obtrusive, but not outright *sneaky.* It's never too early to bring legal advisors into the design process to discuss the best way to present these policies without negatively impacting the user experience.

Square Order's service agreements (Figure 4-13, left) are subtly placed below the email address and password fields on the first screen of its registration flow. Tapping on either of these will bring users to a page in their browser where they can read legal phrases to their heart's content. Square's service agreements are probably the most readable and plain-spoken legal documents you could find. While this subtler approach is the least annoying method and avoids privacy "sticker shock" in the majority of users who don't read this stuff, it runs the risk of users missing the fact that they were ever presented with terms and conditions before signing up.

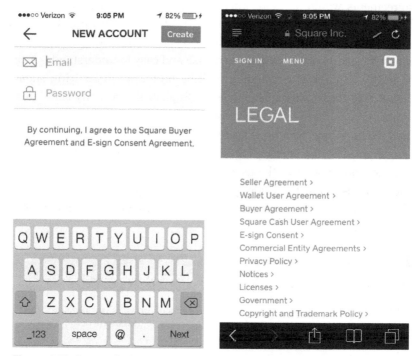

Figure 4-13. Square Order's usage agreements are placed subtly below the registration form, and can be accessed in full via the mobile web browser

PayPal strikes a good balance between transparency and convenience by incorporating the full text of its policies as the last step of its four-step signup flow, but in a way that doesn't force users to read them if they don't want to (Figure 4-14). Dunkin Donuts, on the other hand, is less subtle, dumping the entirety of the document into one long screen that the user must scroll through; the user most likely won't bother to read and will just tap Accept. This approach, while likely meeting the base legal requirements, makes it much harder for users who *do* take the time to read the fine print and inform themselves about the impact an app may have on their privacy.

As designers, we often groan at the idea of having to account for legal statements. This very important content tends to get dismissed (buried in an About menu, or put in a slapdash scrolling view like the Dunkin Donuts example). It's important for designers to keep in mind that users expect to see clear evidence that the payment or banking app they are using adheres to regulatory and legal standards. When it comes to trust in these experiences, the perceived *absence* of service terms and agreements would be more worrisome to the user than the inconvenience of having to tap an extra button. In addition to Terms of Use and privacy statements, at some point in the user's first use of your app you should explain—in a way that is concise and easy to understand—*how* that user's financial information will be protected. Reassuring statements like these can explain in plain English the security standards employed behind the scenes that protect your users' financial information. For example, Venmo (Figure 4-15) reminds users that their data is encrypted each time they log in, while LevelUp calls out its security certifications whenever the user adds a card. Laypeople may not completely understand the underlying encryption protocols at work, but they will have peace of mind that the company that built the app is considerate of their privacy.

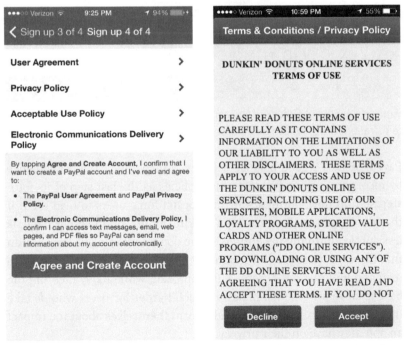

Figure 4-14. Two treatments for the display of Terms of Use statements and privacy policies: PayPal (left), which is thoughtfully organized, and Dunkin Donuts (right), which is not especially easy to read

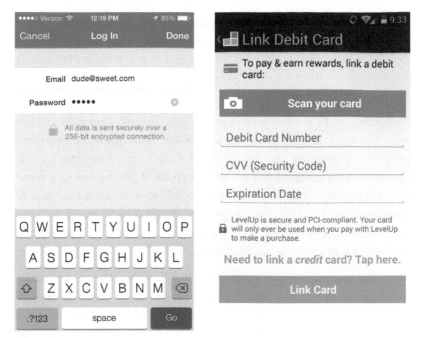

Figure 4-15. Making a point to explain how customer data is secured: Venmo and LevelUp

Security Options: m-PINs, Passcodes, and Passwords

Once users are signed up and ready to start paying with their shiny new mobile wallet, they will want to tap, scan, or check in while feeling in complete control of the experience, trusting in the fact that their financial data is safe. To that end, users will expect a payments app to have basic security features (like PINs or passwords with timed lockouts) and to be able to set display preferences that will work together to maintain their financial privacy.

With any app that handles sensitive financial data, the most familiar security control that users expect to see is a password, passcode, or m-PIN (mobile PIN). An m-PIN screen is a great way to allow users to lock down their app for periods of inactivity, or even as a method to authorize payments—like a digital signature. Passwords associated with a username or other login credential are also useful for this purpose, but the m-PIN format is the most appropriate for the mobile context. It's a familiar interaction, as most mobile devices allow for an additional m-PIN lock or gesture to protect unauthorized use or bring the device out of sleep mode. Numerous reports and surveys on the topic of mobile wallet adoption have found that a mobile PIN lock is the primary security feature that consumers expect to use, and makes them feel most at ease.[11]

Successful m-PIN interfaces should use bespoke keypads, rather than the stock keypad provided by the OS. This prevents nefarious programs (especially on the Android OS) from "listening in" on common touch coordinates for native keypads. It also makes for a more efficient interface if the keypad was designed specifically for the task of entering an m-PIN code (i.e., large touch targets), as opposed to being a calculator-like interface with special characters and mathematic controls that stock OS keypads often display.

The most common design pattern for mobile PINs (Figure 4-16) calls for a large keypad for fast tapping, paired with a grouping of four or five progressive numeric fields that briefly shows the number the user has entered before obscuring it with a dot or asterisk. Additionally, there should be some way for users to recover a lost m-PIN, via a "forgot PIN/passcode" process that resets their m-PIN after they have verified their account through some other means, such as SMS verification code, security questions, or email login.

Isis (Figure 4-16, center) has probably the most successfully designed mobile payment PIN screen to date. It follows the expected pattern closely. The keypad is easy to read, as the numbers are emphasized over the alphabetical characters (which you could argue are not necessary in this context, since the *N* in *PIN* stands for *number*). The keypad is placed in the lower half of the screen, the most comfortable position for one-handed users to reach. Coinbase (Figure 4-16, left) follows this pattern as well, though the user has to tap the Submit button, even after the fields are complete—which is an extra and unnecessary step.

---

11 49% of users surveyed, according to Greg Weed and Mark Sutin, "Credit Card Monitor Q2 2013," Phoenix Marketing International, 2013 (*http://bit.ly/1xNL9sg*).

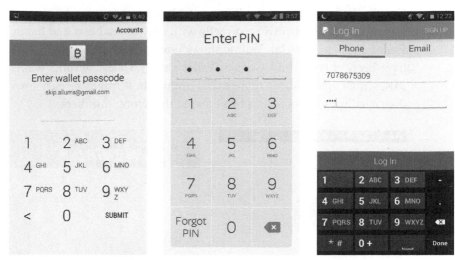

Figure 4-16. Comparison of PIN screens; from left to right: Coinbase, Isis, and PayPal

Meanwhile PayPal (Figure 4-16, right) breaks this pattern, with mixed results. First, PayPal uses default OS keypads, which opens up some vulnerability, especially on the Android platform. Though users have the option of unlocking their app with a PIN as well as their email and password, it requires *more taps* to enter than in apps that use the more common progressive-numeric-field grouping, as the user must also tap an additional Log In button. For entry feedback, the user sees four *tiny* dots entered into the field, which can start to blur together—*wait, how many numbers did I enter?* Lastly, there is nowhere to go if users need help remembering their PIN; they have to switch over to the Email tab and tap the Forgot Password link.

Gracefully handling *incorrect* PIN entries is just as important as making entry of the PIN more efficient. Effective error cases in this regard hinge on two factors. First is the number of incorrect retries. If a four-digit PIN code has four maximum attempts, for example, then there is a .0004% chance that a malicious user could guess your code. That probability increases as the number of maximum attempts does. Second, users should be given clear visual cues and messaging that they have entered their PIN incorrectly, and guided through what to do if they have locked themselves out or forgotten their code.

Google Wallet and Venmo (Figure 4-17) both let users know that they've entered their PIN incorrectly with easy-to-read text and haptic feedback. All good so far. Venmo shows how many incorrect passcodes have been entered, and Google Wallet simply states "Wrong Wallet PIN." In Google Wallet's more subtle approach, it might be easy for a distracted user to not realize he's entered the wrong numbers.

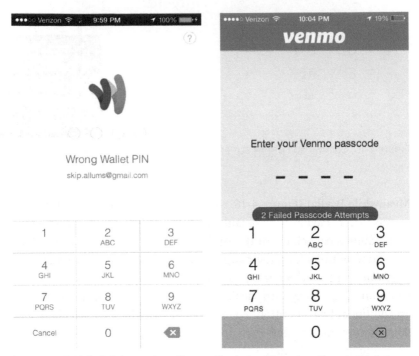

Figure 4-17. Unhelpful error handling methods for PIN entry: Google Wallet (left) and Venmo (right)

Once again, LevelUp excels here (Figure 4-18) by offering helpful negative feedback via flashes of color and cheeky copy without *exactly* revealing the remaining number of attempts. This is a more humanistic way to warn the user than simply stating "Incorrect."

Of course, mobile PINs are not the only way to protect a wallet from unauthorized use. Facial recognition, fingerprint scanning (seen in newer iPhones and Samsung phones), and gestures (like Iugu's QR code–based wallet, shown in Figure 4-19) will soon become prevalent locking mechanisms. We'll look more into the implications these new authorization patterns will have on future wallet interfaces in Chapter 7.

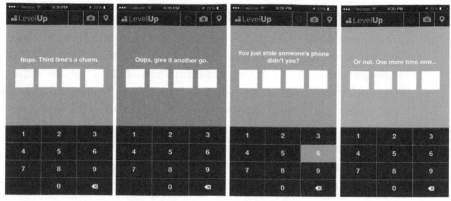

Figure 4-18. LevelUp gives the user several attempts before a final warning, after which she'll be locked out

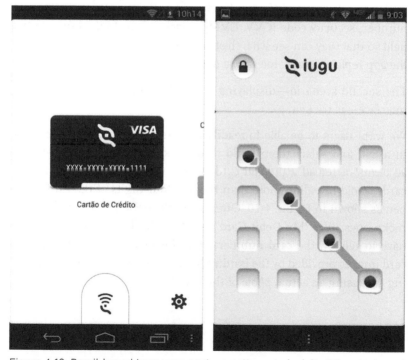

Figure 4-19. Brazil-based Iugu uses gesture patterns to lock its QR code–based wallet

Handling Sensitive Data

Developers should take great care never to expose information about users that would compromise their personal or financial privacy. This includes not only data sets like card numbers and PINs, but also identifiable information like location data, full names, and billing addresses. The easiest way to avoid exposure is not to use them in the first place! This is not really possible, of course. Whether they use closed loop reloadable cards (e.g., Starbucks) or a secure element embedded deep in the phone's innards (e.g., Isis Wallet), all payment apps rely on the user offering up some kind of funding source.

There are two areas in this regard that concern users the most: visual feedback during data entry of their accounts and cards, and the resulting display of those accounts and cards in UI elements. The first scenario is rather straightforward: whenever users enter a credit card number, security code (CVV, CVM), password, or PIN, obfuscate the field so that they can see what they entered for about one second before the app replaces that value with a dot or asterisk.

The second scenario—displaying account information as part of the interface—is trickier.

We want users to be able to readily recognize their accounts or cards in a list, and select them to do things like transfer money between accounts or reload a prepaid card. When displaying credit and debit cards, avoid revealing more than the last four digits of the card number, as shown in Figure 4-20. Offer users the option to give their cards nicknames (like "My Debit Card" or "Gas Card"), so that they don't have to rely on the card number alone for identification. Displaying card images provided by the issuing bank is also helpful, but avoid storing and using an actual *photo* of the card.

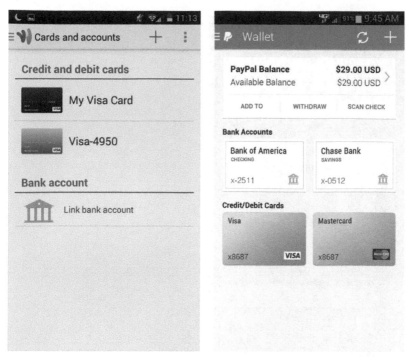

Figure 4-20. Card list views from Google Wallet (left) and PayPal (right) that illustrate how to display a user's cards and accounts without revealing sensitive data

Avoid showing the user's *full* name, either as a greeting at login or under a My Account detail screen, as depicted in Lemon Wallet in Figure 4-21. If there's no business need to display the customer's name, address, or card numbers, then *don't use them*. If it really is necessary, then ensure that such data is stored in a secure hosted service, rather than being hardcoded.[12]

---

12 Lemon Wallet was pulled from the app stores in May 2014 by parent company LifeLock for violation of PCI DSS regulations, most likely for storing this very sensitive information in the user's device memory.

Figure 4-21. A screen from the now-defunct Lemon Wallet, which appears to expose the user's full name, address, birthdate, and ID numbers

Apart from payments and preferences, consumers will also have security worries associated with supplementary services that a mobile wallet may provide, such as location-based offers, maps for nearby merchants, and messaging for transaction events via push notifications or SMS. Again, transparency is the key. Give the user controls, via the Settings menu (Figure 4-22) or when the app is first installed, to opt out of things like sharing location data and push messages. Where possible, explain why the app *needs* access to geolocation data and how it might benefit users (e.g., by helping them find participating merchants and offers that are closest to them).

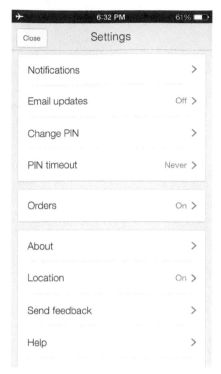

Figure 4-22. Google Wallet allows users to opt out of location and messaging features at any time

The use of transaction histories and alerts is less of a security concern to most users (though you will want to gauge your users' comfort level with testing and surveys). Users generally welcome the idea of being able to keep tabs on when and where their mobile wallet is used, and seeing pending transactions subtracted from their balance (Figure 4-23). Payment alerts and notifications are a useful fraud deterrent, especially if they can also be accessed from other devices or web portals. As money becomes more ethereal in its digital form thanks to services like these, the mobile payment experiences that endure will be the ones that become indispensable to users as spending trackers, helping them to manage their money more wisely.

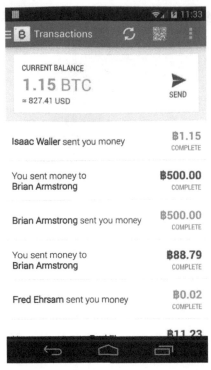

Figure 4-23. Coinbase Wallet transaction history—payment activity should be easy to scan, and clearly show debits, credits, and a current balance whenever possible

Give Them a Helpful Help Section

Finally, provide as much support content as possible. Users will want to go somewhere in the app to find answers to pertinent questions like "What would happen if my phone was stolen?" or "How do I reset my passcode?" This is the most efficient way to provide support to users when they need it, instead of directing them to a website or call center for every issue. Most NFC wallets can be wiped from the device remotely with a simple call to the bank or network operator. Clearly explain contingent processes for scary scenarios like these, and provide direct phone numbers for customer service.

It's likely that your users will have limited experience using their phone to pay for things. It's new cognitive territory, and they are going to have questions about how it all works. They are going to run into situations where the app doesn't work the way they expected (despite your best intentions), so they will look to your app to provide some kind of autonomous support. If you omit this supplementary content, it will leave a bad taste in the user's mouth. Have you ever bought a piece of furniture labeled "some assembly required," and opened the box to find the instructions were missing? Sure, you might have eventually figured out which bolts to put where, but you probably thought twice about ordering something from that retailer again. You don't need to dump your entire functional specification into the Help section, but you should consider including answers for the most likely questions your users would ask.

Avoid marketing speak and technical jargon in these FAQs. Instead, use easy-to-digest, step-by-step guides while maintaining a helpful tone. Here are some examples:

How MyWallet Works:

> **Bad:** "MyWallet is a groundbreaking new way to pay."

> **Worse:** "MyWallet uses the applet instance of your mobile MasterCard that is stored in your UICC SIM, by presenting it to a POS contactless reader accessory via the NFC controller."

> **Better:** "MyWallet uses your NFC-ready phone to securely pay with a MasterCard. When you're ready to pay, simply tap the back of your phone at the register, on the NFC symbol. When you hear the register beep, you're done!"

Users aren't really interested in things like the historical timeline of your company, your mission statement, or your company's Facebook page. They want to know what to do if the app throws an error during a payment, or how to find local merchants that accept the app. This is also a great place to provide animated tutorials or feature walkthroughs that the user would have encountered during the onboarding process.

Structure your help content according to the most common use cases, rather than just replicating the app's architecture. Isis Wallet does a great job of this (Figure 4-24). Its FAQs are grouped into six sections related to the most likely scenarios in which the app would be used (how to pay, where to pay) as well as topics on information security (which Isis refers to as "safety").

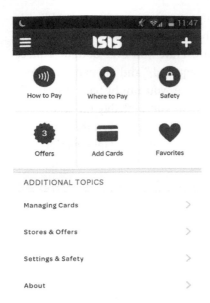

Figure 4-24. Isis Wallet has a robust Help section with FAQs and demos that address topics like how to add cards and what users should do if their phone is lost or stolen

Venmo's Help section (Figure 4-25) breaks down the FAQs into every possible facet of the help subject. It also phrases each FAQ from the user's perspective, demonstrating the thoughtfulness of the support content included here. Venmo has opted to host its FAQs online, making them accessible within the app through a web wrapper. This lets you pivot the Help section by adding more FAQs after launch, as you will no doubt receive customer feedback you may not have anticipated. This way, you don't have to wait until the next release cycle to address support issues your users may be having.

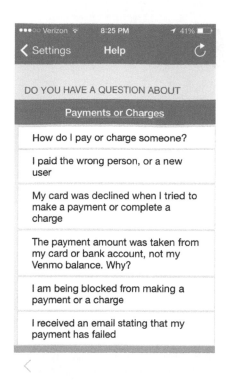

Figure 4-25. Venmo's Help section drills down into most facets of the app, and anticipates potential problem areas or common questions

TabbedOut, on the other hand, has no real in-app support for users who need help with the experience. On its About/Support screen (Figure 4-26), there are several ways to send the company questions (call, email) or connect with it through social media. However, if users are trying to make a purchase and have encountered an issue (like a system time-out error, or if their order hasn't been received by the restaurant), they will likely just give up rather than take the time to write an email describing the issue they are having. They might, however, take the time to slam TabbedOut in their app store reviews or on their Facebook Timelines, since there's not much else to do in its Support section.

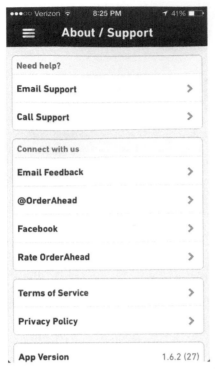

Figure 4-26. TabbedOut's less-than-helpful Support screen

Summary

I admit that the interactions covered in this chapter are not the sexiest. I don't exactly wake up every morning thinking, *Man, I hope I get to design a Terms and Conditions acceptance flow today!* Still, it is challenging to build experiences that hit the right balance of airtight security with empathy for the user who just wants to get in and out of the checkout line with as little stress as possible.

In the course of my day, there tend to be a lot of heated discussions around mobile payment security, and how certain processes we are required to follow might be best practices in the eyes of financial security regulators but are nightmares as user experiences. I often throw the Venn diagram shown in Figure 4-27 into the discussion, as a somewhat sarcastic statement on the state of this relationship.

Figure 4-27. The relationship between security and UX: so close, yet so far away!

The point-of-sale or point-of-decision experience is, of course, paramount in mobile payments, but if these supplementary aspects are not fully realized, potential users will not even *consider* using their phone as a payment tool, much less type their card and bank account numbers into your app's forms, no matter how many parallax animations there are or how much attention you paid to your kerning.

When setting out to change the world of money with your designs, be mindful of these facets that orbit the payment experience. The best analogy to this is buying a car. If your goal is to be able to drive wherever you need to go, would you buy a car that had no seatbelts, no owner's manual, and no locks?

[5]

Designing Successful Payment Interactions

Your user is standing at the register in a grocery store. The cashier rings up her purchases, and a total amount displays on a screen. Your user has pulled out her phone with the intent to pay using your app. What happens next? This is, of course, the crux of mobile payment design, and if the experience is unclear or broken, or simply takes too long, you can bet the user will not give your app a second chance.

Regardless of the method you utilize, the most important factors to keep in mind when plotting out your payment flow are time and effort. In the context of a shopping experience, the window during which a payment at the register happens is relatively tiny, compared with all the effort users expend in the process of purchasing something. A task analysis of a typical shopping trip reveals five phases: planning, travel, browsing, purchase, and completion (Figure 5-1). Each phase has its own set of tasks that users must complete to reach their end goal—buying groceries, for example.

When designing your checkout experience, consider the cost of user effort with the timing of these tasks, in context with all the other steps users have to take to get to this point, and think about how those previous tasks might influence their mindset. Are they annoyed because they waited in a long line? Did they find everything they wrote down on their shopping list? How many bus transfers did they make in order to get to the grocery store? In terms of mental and physical effort, the payment experience should rank near the lower end of the scale, with the least amount of friction possible.

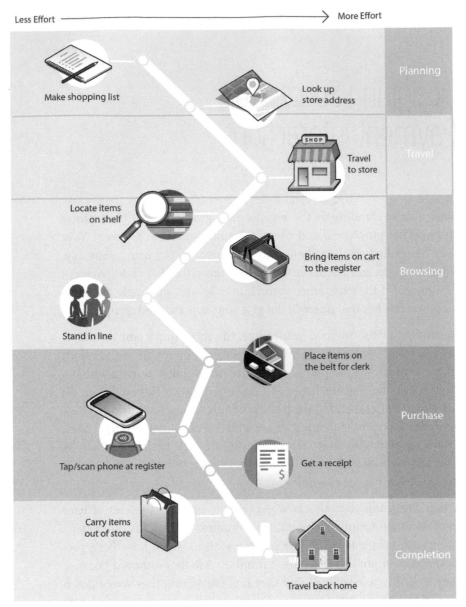

Figure 5-1. A typical mobile payment customer journey in the brick-and-mortar retail world, and the effort required in each phase of the shopping trip

Mobile payments are not meant to be complex, engrossing, and experiential—like games or social interactions. They should be lightning-quick and dead simple; otherwise, your app will just get in the way of your users enjoying or using whatever it is they set out to buy. It's important to remember that interacting with your app is never the user's end goal.

This chapter will focus on designing successful mobile interactions at the point of sale, using the three most popular payment methods: NFC, QR (quick response) codes and 2D barcodes, and geolocation. Table 5-1 shows the UX benefits and challenges of the three frameworks we will explore, and which live apps you can refer to as examples of the respective technologies in action (they are covered in depth in Chapters 3 and 4).

TABLE 5-1. A comparison of the three mobile payment interactions

FRAMEWORK	BENEFITS	CHALLENGES	EXAMPLES
NFC	Transaction speed, no need for data network, high security	Merchant adoption, user education	Isis, Google Wallet
Barcodes and QR codes	Works on most devices and OSes	Dependence on data connectivity, lack of security standards, merchant acceptance	Starbucks, LevelUp
Geolocation	Works on most devices and OSes, less effort for the user to pay	Dependence on data connectivity and GPS accuracy, user education	PayPal

Near Field Communication (NFC)

NFC presents a whole new mode for consumers to use their mobile devices, in which they can interact with their physical environment (tags, other NFC-enabled devices) instead of being passive "receivers of information" via their phones. NFC lets mobile users tap to initiate a short-range data transfer. NFC technology can be used to open a door, pay a transit fare, or swap contact details and pictures.

Apart from the novelty of bumping phones together, NFC offers many other advantages, like being built on well-established global security standards and simplifying the redemption of loyalty cards and coupons. The latter feature appeals especially to retail marketers that wish to drive up redemption rates of their promotional programs, and explains the recent buzz around large mobile operators and device manufacturers partnering with financial institutions to put a stake in the ground of mobile wallets. This model will only become more prevalent given the growing numbers of new NFC-enabled Android, Windows, and BlackBerry phones shipping—nearly 235 million in 2013.[1] For a more in-depth look at how NFC works behind the scenes, refer back to the profile of the NFC ecosystem in Chapter 2.

Because NFC is largely dependent on hardware, and has a variety of usage patterns (authorize and tap, versus Tap & Go without opening the app), designers must create obvious feedback patterns for when the phone taps a reader, and the outcome of the payment. NFC payments also require more instructional cues than 2D barcode/QR code- or geolocation-based apps, as many users are not familiar with how NFC works. The last thing a user wants is to get to the register and fruitlessly bonk their phone on the point-of-sale with no apparent results, holding up the checkout line.

NFC ESSENTIALS

Because NFC is such an underutilized technology (especially to US users), a payment interaction with this method lives and dies by the visual and haptic cues given to the user throughout the experience: how to pay, when the phone is ready to pay, and when the payment is done. It's key to give users clear directions and calls to action, and keep them informed of what is going on. With NFC, the actual data exchange (between the phone and the point of sale) is literally half a second, so there's little room (or need) for lengthy transitions or complex animations at each interaction point. These three interactions are:

1. Initiating a payment

2. Tapping the phone on the reader

3. Receiving the payment result

Besides your app, the user will also encounter a variety of audible and visual stimuli that will be out of your purview, as there are several NFC reader manufacturers. No two NFC readers will look exactly the same, and the sounds or visual feedback they provide the user will vary (see Figure 5-2 for examples from some of the major providers in this space:

---

1 "NFC Devices, Strategies, and Form Factors: Update and Roadmap," ABI Research, 2013 (*http://bit.ly/VVWKbB*).

VeriFone, First Data, and Vivotech). The screens you design for this experience will be the one constant as the user moves from store to store, tapping away, so it pays[2] to create a payment flow that is meaningful and reliable. So let's explore the three interaction points in more depth.

Figure 5-2. Three examples of NFC readers found at the retail point of sale; there are a handful of manufacturers that merchants can choose from, and no two are strictly alike in terms of interface design

Initiate a payment

The first step is providing a very prominent button (e g , Pay) or status indicator (e.g., Ready to Pay) so the user doesn't have to speculate about how to start the transaction. The nature of UI messaging here really depends on the particular implementation, and allows for the following distinct conditions:

Tap & Go
> Payments can be made whenever the device is on. The app doesn't need to be open to pay.

Open & Tap
> Payments can be made as long as the app is open, and one of the mobile cards is turned on.

---

2 Apologies for this pun, dear reader, but you must give me credit for waiting until you were halfway through the book to use it.

Tap on Demand

Payments can be made only when the user opens the app and manually turns a mobile card on, and only for a brief window of time (e.g., less than 30 seconds).

An obvious, actionable path here will start the payment experience off on the right foot. For a good example of this first step, have a look at Google Wallet, which uses the Open & Tap method. It shows a large blue box that clearly reads "You're ready to tap & pay" under the card the user has selected. For payment apps using a Tap & Go implementation, users don't even need to open their app to pay—NFC payments are always on. In this case, you'll want to show clear controls when the app is open that indicate when the user's NFC app is on or off. For apps using Tap on Demand, all that's really needed is a large button that reads Pay or Pay Now placed in the center of the lower half of the screen, which is the most comfortable ergonomic location for one-handed use. For Tap & Go and Open & Tap methods, it's a good idea to include the contactless payment symbol (which resembles the Wi-Fi "waves" icon turned on its side) most likely to be found on the face of NFC readers, so that the user can associate your app with compatible point-of-sale registers. Refer to Table 5-2 for some examples of action buttons for these three payment modes.

TABLE 5-2. Three call-to-action button examples for the respective NFC payment modes

TAP & GO	OPEN & TAP	TAP ON DEMAND
))) NFC Pay: On	Ready to Pay)))	Pay

Tap the phone on the reader

Use purposeful animations to alert users that a payment event is occurring, like a pulsating "halo" around the card they have selected, or animating the contactless "wave" symbol. This should be supplemented by haptic or audio cues to tell the user when a payment source has come in contact with a compatible reader. As many users are still unfamiliar with how NFC works, it may be necessary to specify that they tap the *back* of the phone on the reader. (In usability testing sessions I have observed, 30% of participants in the US had no idea where the NFC antenna in their phones was located.) You can do this by showing a diagram of how best to present the phone to the reader. If your app uses Tap on Demand, a large timer should be displayed to count down the seconds until the mobile NFC card will be turned off. When using the Open & Tap or Tap & Go method, you will want to notify the user that a tap has been detected, and that the results of that tap are coming soon. Figure 5-3 shows two examples of how these visual elements can work together to clearly communicate to a user that the payment is in progress.

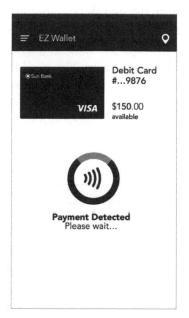

Figure 5-3. Payment prompts for Tap & Go/Open & Tap mode (left) versus Tap on Demand mode (right)

Receive the payment result

Once the user's phone has been read by the NFC reader, the next step is to clearly indicate to the user that the tap was successful, or that something has gone wrong, as the case may be. Account for this by using a screen that clearly shows the outcome of the payment, and rein-force that outcome with short vibration pulses or audio cues. If the NFC reader at the register doesn't beep or light up, it's possible the reader is off, broken, or not compatible (some shops may have old or faulty readers at their registers, oblivious to their working condition). Keep in mind that NFC readers vary in the strength of their NFC fields, so some readers may recognize a tap from inches away, while for others the phone must physically *touch* the reader pad (especially if the particular phone has a protective case). Lots can go wrong!

If the tap was successful, show the user the outcome relevant to the card he has selected. Some NFC readers used in South America, Europe, and Asia may be able to send back to the phone the metadata around a transaction (e.g., the amount and the name of the merchant), so include those details if possible to make the payment feedback as rich as possible. You will also need to inform the user if there are additional actions needed to finish the payment. For example, the user's bank may have enforced a limit on the amount of purchases (e.g., any over $100) that he can make with his mobile card, so you may need to allow the user to authorize the payment with his m-PIN. This is meant to protect the user from theft or unauthorized use of his card. Table 5-3 shows some examples of possible NFC payment outcomes, and what stimuli should be offered back to the user.

TABLE 5-3. Possible transaction outcomes from interacting with NFC readers

PAYMENT OUTCOME	FEEDBACK TO THE USER
Payment accepted	**PAYMENT SUCCESSFUL** $15.99 *paid from:* Visa Card ...5678 Home Depot *[one short vibration pulse]*
Refund processed	**REFUND** $20.00 *refunded to:* Visa Card ...5678 *[one short vibration pulse]*
Payment declined	**PAYMENT DECLINED** Please select another card and try again. *[two short vibration pulses]*

Reader not working/not supported	**PAYMENT INCOMPLETE** This reader may not be working properly. Please check with the merchant and try again. *[one long vibration pulse]*
User authentication required	**m-PIN REQUIRED** Amount: $100.00 Please enter your m-PIN to authorize this purchase. *[three short vibration pulses]*

The best way to learn about this or any payment technology is to use it yourself. I would also encourage you to sign up for any NFC wallet service available to you, use it for a week or so at a variety of stores, and get a feel for how NFC phones and readers in general interact with one another. Think about how *you* might improve a particular mobile wallet's experience. Table 5-4 gives a sampling of NFC payment initiatives, listed by country (as of this writing).

TABLE 5-4. NFC wallets around the world

US	CANADA	FRANCE	GERMANY	SOUTH KOREA	SINGAPORE	JAPAN
• Isis • Google Wallet	• Royal Bank of Canada • CIBC • Tim Hortons	• Cityzi • Orange Cash • BNP Paribas KIX	• O2 Wallet • mpass	• KFTC BankWallet • Cashbee • LG PayNow	• SingTel mWallet • StarHub SmartWallet • M1	• DoCoMo Osaifu-Keitai • Japan Rail East Suica

PUTTING IT ALL TOGETHER

Now let's take a look at some typical NFC payment scenarios, and see how the three steps (initiation, the tap, the result) work together. For this book, I've put together some flow diagrams and basic wireframe concepts to illustrate each step.

The first one, shown in Figure 5-4, is a user flow for a Tap on Demand payment. Here the user must first intentionally activate a payment by tapping a button (1), such as Pay or On, which will turn on the mobile card for a brief interval of time. A countdown timer displays, and the user is prompted to hold her phone over the NFC reader (2). Once the payment is complete (3), the app lets the user know with vibration pulses or audio cues, accompanied by the amount of the purchase, the name of the merchant (when possible), and the card that was used.

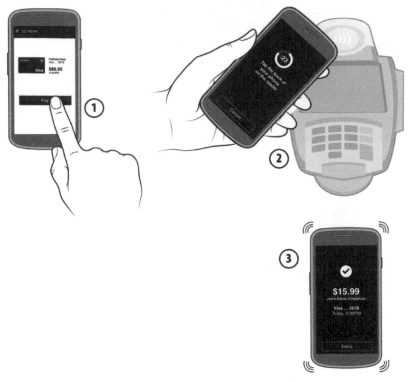

Figure 5-4. An NFC payment using Tap on Demand mode

In the case of Open & Tap (Figure 5-5), the app is ready to pay as long as the phone is powered on and the app is open. The user doesn't need to do all that much—she can pay simply by holding the phone over the NFC reader. When the reader is detected by the phone (1), an animation shows that a payment is in progress, followed shortly by the payment confirmation (2) and haptic and audio cues.

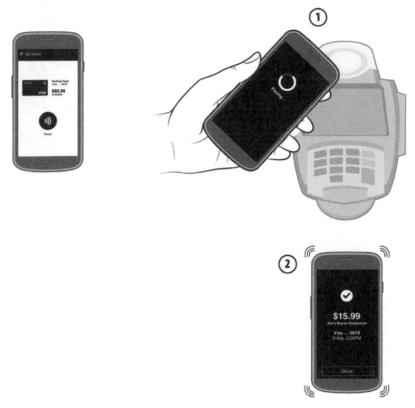

Figure 5-5. An NFC payment using Open & Tap mode

Tap & Go payments, as shown in Figure 5-6, offer a payment mode ideally suited for transit use cases, because it requires the least amount of effort from the user; she may not even have to unlock her phone's screen. When she approaches the turnstile, the user simply taps her phone on the gate's NFC reader pad as she passes through (1). The phone vibrates or dings, letting her know her phone has been read (2). You should make use of the OS notification drawer and any lock-screen messaging capabilities to notify the user of any taps that have happened since she last looked at her phone. When the user eventually unlocks her screen, show her a payment confirmation screen (3).

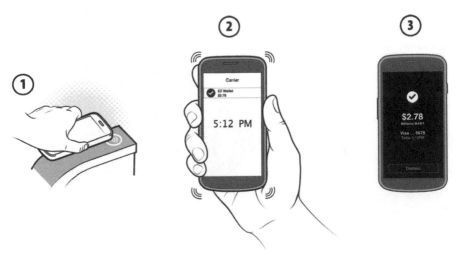

Figure 5-6. An NFC payment using Tap & Go mode in a transit scenario

There may be times when the user will be required to authorize a payment by entering her m-PIN. This multistep process applies when the user attempts a payment that is over a threshold set by her issuing bank (such as a high dollar amount), to protect against unauthorized payments. First, the user taps her phone on the reader (1). The app shows the total amount of the purchase, and asks for the user's m-PIN (2). The user enters her m-PIN (3) and taps the phone on the reader again (4), and now the payment is processed (5). This scenario is a little less convenient than a normal NFC tap, but goes a long way toward reassuring the user that her mobile cards are always protected from theft. This scenario is shown in Figure 5-7.

There may be times when the reader is not working or configured properly, or does not accept the tap for some reason. In this case (Figure 5-8), when the user taps her phone (1), the payment result (2) should include obvious alert iconography, messaging written in plain language should describe the error, and the user should be given options to retry or cancel the payment.

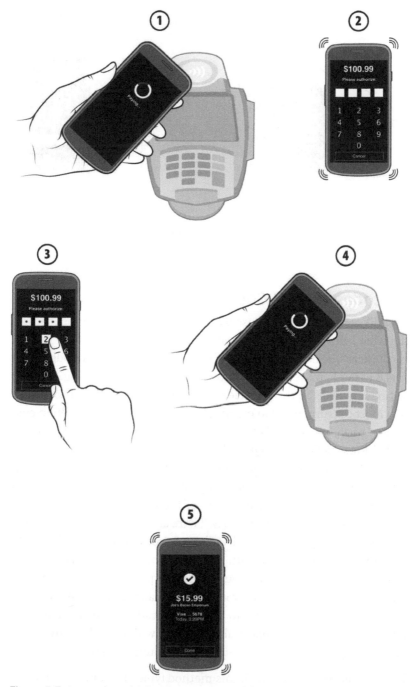

Figure 5-7. Approving a high-value payment with an m-PIN

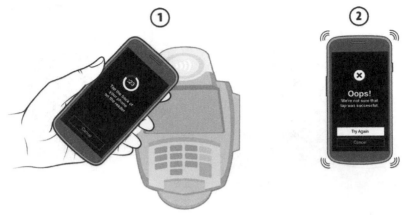

Figure 5-8. A miscommunication or error during interaction with the POS reader

Barcodes and QR Codes

Apps like Starbucks, which use barcodes and QR codes, are fast becoming what I like to call the "gateway drug" of mobile payments. That is, consumers who have become comfortable with using 2D barcodes often find it easier to move on to NFC, geolocation, remote ordering, or other payment models. In the US, at least, Starbucks is the first real exposure that most consumers get to mobile payments, with over 10 million customers providing about 11% of the company's revenue. Resembling a digital Rorschach image, QR codes can be encoded with data that will direct POS scanners to charge a registered account or a prepaid card. This method is generally faster to implement than NFC wallets, though it is less secure due to the exposure of the user's payment source on screen in the form of a visual proxy. There are no encryption standards for barcode- or QR code–based wallets, so codes can be vulnerable to theft or interception. Still, with emerging concepts like tokenization, barcodes and QR codes may have a shot at supplanting NFC as the most secure method of mobile payments. The major card companies like Visa and MasterCard have yet to issue specifications that endorse these methods per se, but it's conceivable that they will, should tokenized 2D codes emerge as the frontrunner for the consumer market.

Point-of-sale experiences with this method typically require the user to either align his phone's screen with a POS scanner (held by the merchant or fixed to the register), or alternately use his phone's camera to scan a code generated and presented by the merchant. Accounting for these two distinct interactions, successful designs should facilitate fast scanning while addressing user's security concerns and need for feedback from the payment experience.

BARCODE AND QR CODE ESSENTIALS

Regardless of whether your app is designed for consumer- or merchant-presented codes, you should adhere closely to the following best practices, which call for optimized scanning of the code images and efficient user feedback.

Show me the code

Display the barcode or QR code as soon as the app is launched. Don't bury it under a subscreen or behind a Pay button. If the user is opening his app in a store with the intent to pay, the last thing he wants is to have to hunt for where his code is so he can show it to the merchant. LevelUp is a great example of this. However, if your app's architecture or business rules can't allow for this (payments are a smaller aspect of a larger wallet-like experience), try to make navigating to the code as efficient as possible. You might consider looking at using geolocation services like GPS or Bluetooth Low Energy beacons to determine whether a consumer happens to be at or near a participating merchant, so you can bring up his code when the context of use is most appropriate.

Secure the code

QR codes and barcodes are generally not secure, so dynamically generating codes using a tokenization method can help reduce the risk of exposing account details. For example, the data attached to the code could be refreshed after five transactions, making the old code obsolete and reducing the risk of a thief duplicating or redirecting the QR code somewhere else. You may also provide a security option, such as an m-PIN or password lock, to further prevent unauthorized use.

Create big codes

Make the QR code or barcode on screen as large as possible to make for a better scanning target. For example, the Gyft app for mobile gift cards forces the screen into landscape mode, to provide lots of screen real estate for displaying a linear barcode. The Starbucks app for Android uses this method as well. However, for consumer-presented codes, don't scale the image *so* wide that the merchant has trouble scanning it, as most retail POS registers are equipped only with short-range readers. A needlessly wide barcode may force an awkward dance where the checkout cashier has to increase her distance from your user's screen in order to fit the code to her scanner's laser field.

Use the best light and high contrast

If possible, override the consumer device's current screen brightness setting temporarily to display at the brightest level. This is a device attribute that is exposed to developers by various OS platforms, so check with your target platforms' developer guides for the best method to accomplish this. You should refer to the Starbucks app for an example of this in practice. To mitigate any screen glare from sunlight or environmental light, stick to high-contrast, black-and-white code images. Try to resist the temptation to incorporate custom colors or images within the code pattern. Participating merchants may not be using newer multiangle optical scanners (Figure 5-9), and anything but a conventional barcode or QR code might stump them. As an illustration of this, think back to when you have seen a checkout cashier struggle to scan a barcode label on an item that was round and packed in rumpled plastic.

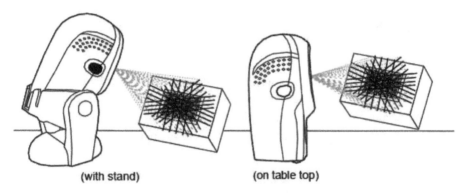

(with stand)   (on table top)

Figure 5-9. A typical short-range barcode scanner, courtesy of Motorola

Use camera guides

Depending on whether your app supports scanning merchant barcodes or QR codes, you will want to help your user align the code image correctly for scanning, using a viewfinder-style box or guidelines on the scanning screen. This will help the user quickly orient the camera to the right position to get an accurate read, and eliminate guesswork.

Provide rapid payment feedback

Once the user has presented his code to the merchant (or read the merchant's code) with his app, the next aspect is payment feedback. The user will expect to be informed whether the payment was successful, and to see some form of digital receipt that captures the amount, the name of the merchant, and perhaps an itemized receipt. To facilitate this feedback, communications between the merchant's POS system, the web service your app uses to settle the transaction, and the user's phone need to be as efficient as possible. Otherwise, the user will have to rely on the merchant telling him whether the payment was accepted, which is sufficient, but not a new experience. This is especially true for closed loop wallets that rely on a stored-value card (like a gift card) to fund the transaction; the user will need a way to keep track of the current balance.

PUTTING IT ALL TOGETHER

Now let's take a look at some typical payment scenarios that use image codes, and see how the user experience elements I've outlined come together. Here are two user flows, one for a consumer-presented QR code, and one for a merchant-presented barcode.

In Figure 5-10, the user's app is displaying a QR code that links to her funding source. This could be a stored-value card (e.g., gift card, prepaid card) or a debit or credit card. The scanner at the point of sale picks up the QR code pattern and processes the payment (1). Shortly afterward, the app should display a notification that the payment has completed successfully (2).

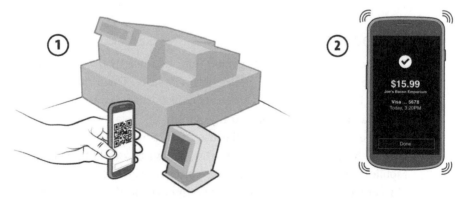

Figure 5-10. The consumer presenting a QR code to a scanner at the point of sale

In Figure 5-11, the consumer must scan the code displayed at the point of sale by the merchant. To do this, the consumer must find the QR code with her phone's camera and align it inside a set of guidelines (1). Once the code is read and the payment has been received by the merchant, a notification displays the outcome (2).

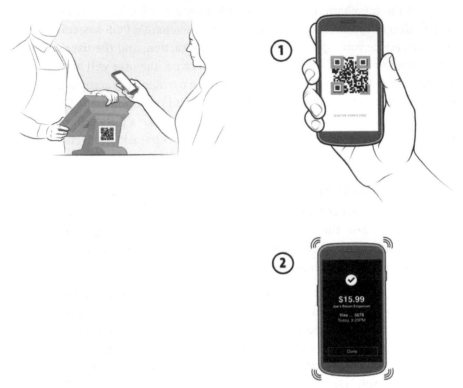

Figure 5-11. A consumer scanning a merchant's QR code at checkout

Geolocation

Think of payments using geolocation technology like having an invisible fence around the perimeter of a store. Once the consumer crosses into this perimeter, the merchant is made aware of his presence, facilitating the opportunity for a financial exchange. This could be negotiated through the use of GPS or BLE (Bluetooth Low Energy) beacons, depending on the target devices you'd like to support. Mobile payment apps that use geolocation are significant in their *lack* of interactions, because there is less emphasis on the communication between hardware components as the conduit for a purchase (as seen in the NFC model). Payments in this mode don't even require the user to pull out his phone if the merchant has been indicated by the user as a "favorite." Apps like now-defunct Square Wallet and PayPal are designed to work "in the background," so that a user needs only to open the door of his favorite café to open a tab. The user has a payment source stored in a secure cloud service, which can be charged only if he crosses the merchant's geofence, or manually makes himself known to the merchant by checking in. With Square in particular, these types of transactions resemble the days when you could walk into your local corner store, and the store owner would know you by name. If you didn't have any cash on you, you could simply put your bill on a running tab to be settled later.

GEOLOCATION PAYMENT ESSENTIALS

Designing for this experience is primarily driven by efficiently allowing the user to find nearby participating merchants, making transaction preference settings easy to understand, and offering the user clear feedback once his payment has been processed.

Find a store

First, ensure that searching for shops is as fluid as possible, as this payment experience relies on the user finding participating merchants *before* he enters the store. This means using mobile location search patterns (including map view, list view, and distance and directions to the nearest merchant) to direct the user to a participating merchant. After all, the user can't pay if he can't find the store in the first place. Make the store search feature a prominent option of your app's menu, so that the user can pull it up whenever he intends to use the app.

Authorize payment easily

Consider how the user will want to initiate and authorize a purchase when he doesn't have to hand over a traditional form of payment (like cash or a card). There are typically two patterns for initiating a payment in this type of experience:

Automatic authorization

> If the user is within range of the store, he can "check in" (intentionally or by remembering a favorite merchant) in order to make himself known to the merchant POS system. When the merchant "sees" the user in its system, it can then charge a bill to that user,

and a digital receipt should be sent a few seconds later. The user's mere presence in the store is enough to establish that he will accept any charges the merchant bills to him. This method is great for speeding up checkout lines, and can be seen in PayPal, when a PayPal register merchant "sees" a user pop up on its screen and charges the bill to the user. In this case, time is of the essence, so system speed should support expedient communication by the geo-location service that notifies the merchant that the user is checked in, the billing service that charges the transaction to the user, and the notification method to confirm to the user that the payment was received. Lag in any of these communications will give the impression that "something" is not working, causing unwanted confusion at the register.

Manual authorization

If the user has checked in to a store, and the merchant charges a bill to that user, there could be an extra step that gives the user the opportunity to review an itemized bill before accepting the charges. After confirming that he is happy with the bill, the user can authorize the payment by pressing a Confirm or Check Out button. He may also want to add a tip to the bill. This method is great for those users for whom security is of the utmost concern, and previewing any charges made to their account gives them more control of the experience. Manual authorization may call for more system communication steps than the automatic method, meaning the speed of the overall interaction may be slightly longer, so this option may not be best for stores with high volumes of customer traffic.

Provide rapid payment feedback

As with the other payment experiences, prompt feedback is critical in making the user comfortable in the stability of this new way of paying. As any visual feedback or payment confirmation in the form of a digital receipt or a bill must be delivered via data networks or Wi-Fi, it's key to make the web services necessary to deliver transaction confirmations as agile as possible, whether by text, push notifications, or in-app messaging. Users won't want to wait more than 5 or 10 seconds for some kind of payment confirmation; any longer than that, and they'll start to wonder where their money is going. This applies regardless of whether the feedback is generic (e.g., "Payment received!") or an itemized digital bill for which the user must approve the total amount. Users will also expect to see the name and location of the merchant who charged them, to alleviate any concerns of theft or misuse.

PUTTING IT ALL TOGETHER

Now let's take a look at three interactions with geolocation for payments, and see how the three user touchpoints (locating a store, authorizing a payment, providing feedback) work together for a seamless payment experience.

Figure 5-12 shows an automatic authorization geolocation scenario. First, the user searches for the nearby merchant where she wishes to pay with the app. Once the user enters a merchant's location, she can check in (1, 2) to make herself known to the merchant's POS system. The merchant will see the user pop up on its list of current customers, and can then charge a bill to the user's account (3). The user receives a notification on her phone when the purchase is done (4).

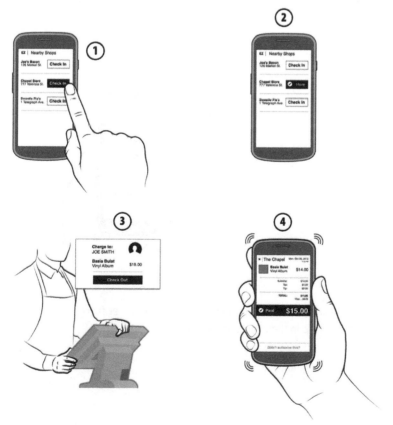

Figure 5-12. Checking in to a shop to pay

For stores that the user visits often, she may elect to set a particular store as a favorite so that the app will automatically check her in whenever she's within range. This preference is reflected in Figure 5-13. This option (1) saves the step of the user having to open her app and manually check in every time. Otherwise, the process is the same: the user arrives at the store (2), the merchant sees the user pop up on the POS system, and the merchant charges a bill to the user (3).

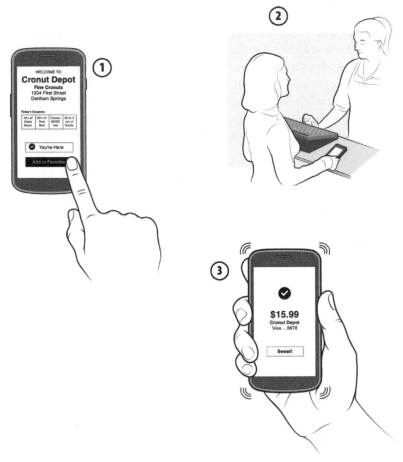

Figure 5-13. Allowing a user to automatically check in to her favorite nearby store can save a step in the checkout process

In manual authorization cases (see Figure 5-14), users will want to review the bill the merchant has charged them before authorizing the sale. For this interaction, when bill is sent to the user's app (1), she will expect to press a button labeled Authorize or Pay (2), then receive a confirmation message (3). Tips can be added as well; ideally, the app would give the user preset tip amounts or percentages to eliminate the guesswork of figuring out appropriate tip amounts.

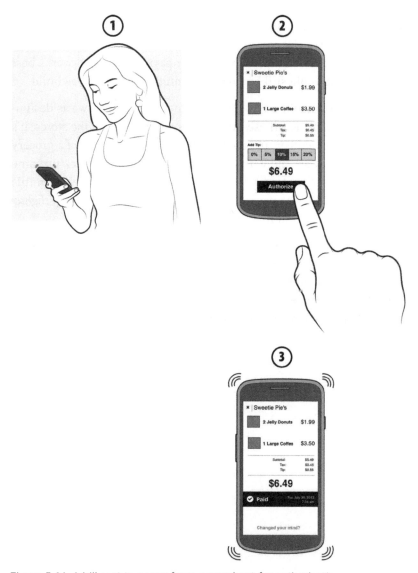

Figure 5-14. A bill sent to a user from a merchant for authorization

Summary

It's hard at the outset to judge whether nascent payment technologies, like the ones described in this chapter, will have any significant impact on social and commercial interactions. It may seem especially hazy now, with so many ecosystem players and newfangled gadgets coming out every week that claim to disrupt the world of payments as we know it. What is clear to me is that the way we earn, save, and use our money is most certainly being revolutionized by the sum of all these different initiatives. I can't say which will be the undisputed winner (NFC, QR codes, or whatever else comes next), and there may *never* be a clear winner, as users will be drawn to whichever payment method works best for them. That might still be cash. That might be the app *you* build.

As the world of mobile payments continues to broil, and we as designers begin to shape how these experiences will play out in the stores, it's important to remember that the goal of a user in the midst of a grocery run is *not* to play around with your app. He just wants to pick up some ribeyes, get home, and grill them for his family. Still, your work in this space adds value to the user's life by making that shopping trip *slightly* faster, and his payment methods safer from fraud.

This kind of service design revolution is unprecedented, and the technology enabling this change is truly groundbreaking (if not a little frustrating at times) and continues to mature every day. Still, the fundamental UX principles (like efficiency, feedback, and context) included in this chapter will remain relevant.

[6]

Adding Value with Peripheral Services

Jerry Seinfeld: *Your back hurts because of your wallet. It's huge!*
George Costanza: *This isn't just my wallet. It's an organizer, a memory, and an old friend.*
Jerry: *Your friend is obese.*

—*Seinfeld*, Season 9, Episode 12, "The Reverse Peephole"

Who are you designing a mobile payment experience for: a George, a Jerry, or another customer altogether? When you're approaching a mobile wallet and payments solution, it can be challenging to nail down the right key features desired by your user base. Commerce and retail is an obvious starting point, but the concept of a "wallet" means different things to different people. Some people keep only a few credit cards, a debit card, and an ID in their wallet. Others follow the George Costanza model: a wallet overflowing with their payment cards, paper bills, small change, an archive of receipts, loyalty stamp cards from local shops, forgotten coupons, and more. What is common to most definitions of the "mobile wallet" is that it is something that is personal, private, and useful for everyday tasks. When defining and vetting the features that your users will want from a payment solution, you must decide how closely your product should mirror the various mental models of this very personal carry-all. Do your app's customers desire a "Swiss Army knife" for all things related to their money? Or do they just need a wallet to be a giant Buy or Pay button? I am of the mind that consumers are not only looking for a tool that helps them spend *faster*, they expect a set of mobile tools that will work *in concert* with payments to help them spend *smarter*—staying on top of their cash flow and making informed financial decisions.

In South Louisiana, where I grew up, we practice the Creole concept of *lagniappe*. It means, roughly, "a little something extra," and it was born out of shop owners giving their customers a small free gift with their purchase—for example, a drink or pieces of candy for the shopper's children.[1] There was a café in my hometown that would give you a free café au lait if you bought two beignets,[2] which made it a local favorite. Likewise, in order to encourage adoption, mobile wallets must offer more than just the gimmick of paying for goods with one's phone using whichever technology is the flavor of the month; they need some kind of enticing and supplementary lagniappe to get consumers to switch to a new way of paying from the cards and cash they know and love. Whether the lagniappe comes in the form of over-the-air savings, convenient financial tools, or digital travel dossiers, mobile wallets should endeavor to be indispensable: little personal assistants that make the small but important tasks in the consumer's daily life easier.

A Day in the Life of a Mobile Wallet User

To illustrate the versatility and usefulness of what a well-designed mobile wallet could be, let's walk through a set of day-in-the-life use cases that reflect a world in which leaving the house without an analog wallet would not ruin your day.

1. Heading in to work shortly after 8 a.m., I walk down to the BART (Bay Area Rapid Transit) station. As I walk, I launch the EZ Wallet app on my phone and check the train times. The Pittsburg/Bay Point train is running a few minutes late, as usual. I check the balance on my Clipper card. It's a bit low ($2.50) since it's the end of the week, so I press the Reload button and choose to transfer $50 over from my linked bank account. The Clipper balance refreshes to show a new total of $52.50 (see Figure 6-1), enough to cover my transportation costs for the next week. At the station, I tap my phone on the turnstile. The phone vibrates in my hand, the gate opens, and a notification pops up: "MacArthur BART, ON." I head up the stairs to the platform and catch the 8:20 train. I get

---

1 Mark Twain, *Life on the Mississippi* (Boston: James R. Osgood & Co., 1883), Chapter 44 (*http://bit.ly/1qVnwNR*).

2 A deep-fried puff pastry covered in powdered sugar, made famous in New Orleans by Café Du Monde in the French Quarter.

off at Montgomery Street Station in the San Francisco Financial District, and tap my phone on the turnstile on the way out. My phone buzzes again: "Montgomery St. Station, OFF—$3.35."

Figure 6-1. A transit scenario: looking up train schedules, reloading a prepaid account, and tapping a phone at the entry gate

2. On the way out I stop at the Peet's Coffee stand for my morning latte. My wallet app knows I am near Peet's, so when I open it the Peet's Card is the first thing I see. I click the Pay button, and the card spins around and reveals a QR code, which I show to the barista and she scans. The screen refreshes to show that $3.50 was removed from my Peet's Card balance, as well as a note that this was my 10th consecutive latte, so the next one is free! (See Figure 6-2.) I ride up the escalator to the street, hot latte in hand.

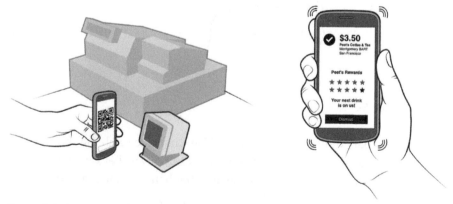

Figure 6-2. Receiving rewards points for repeat purchases

3. Down on Brannan Street, I arrive at the lobby of my company's building. A BLE (Bluetooth Low Energy) beacon picks up my mobile device as I walk through the front door. As I pass the security gate, the doorperson at the desk sees my face, name, company, and access status pop up on her screen, and waves me through.

4. At lunch, a coworker tells me that one of my favorite singers, Canadian folk artist Basia Bulat, is on tour and is playing tonight at The Chapel, a San Francisco music venue. I pull up the venue's website and buy a ticket for the show. A minute or two later, I get an email with the ticket and a barcode, which I save to my wallet app. (See Figure 6-3.)

Figure 6-3. Adding an e-ticket to the wallet

5. That evening, I head down to The Chapel to catch the show. At the door, the venue's BLE beacon wakes up my wallet app and pulls up my ticket. I show the barcode to the bouncer. He scans the ticket, and I'm in.

6. The Basia Bulat concert is a fun one. She is performing several songs from her new album, which was just released on vinyl this week. After the show is over, I stop by the merchandise table to pick up a copy. There is a sign for EZ Wallet checkout. I open up the

app, click Nearby Shops, select The Chapel, and click the Check In button. When I get to the front of the line, I ask for the new album on vinyl. The salesperson recognizes my face from his tablet app's Current Customers list, and asks, "Are you Skip?" I answer "Yes," and he touches my avatar, charging my account $15 for the album. My phone buzzes with a notification: "$15 paid at The Chapel." I bid goodnight to my friends and head back to BART.

These use cases are not so far fetched—they can be accomplished today, thanks to the many innovations inherent in mobile technology. First-world countries like South Korea, Japan, and Germany (see Figure 6-4) have been using their mobile phones for these very tasks for a decade. What are they using them for? A survey of the Japanese mobile wallet market showed the following spending categories spread over 9.8 million users: 80% retail, 32% vending machines, 30% public transport, 29% groceries, and 15% restaurants.[3] Those five verticals have fairly unique retail interactions: small payments at vending machines and transit being impersonal experiences, and the rest requiring face-to-face interactions with merchants for larger purchases.

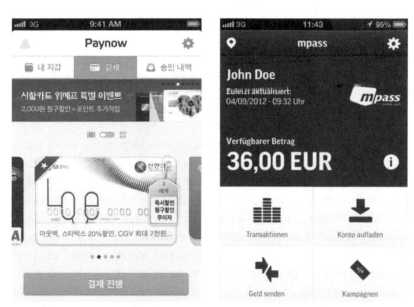

Figure 6-4. Two mobile wallets, from South Korea (left) and Germany (right)

---

3 "Mobile Year in Review 2010," ComScore MobiLens, February 2011.

It's Not Just About Payments

The potential for mobile wallets extends far beyond retail or financial use cases. Anything that consumers carry in a wallet—receipts, coupons, plane tickets, health insurance ID cards, or door keys—could be digitized and consolidated into one mobile experience, in an effort to help users accomplish these tasks more efficiently and without having to carry around disparate papers or cards that are easily misplaced. This content could fall under many umbrellas: banking, commerce, or even identity and access. Figure 6-5 is a fair visualization of what kinds of content could be enfolded into a mobile wallet.

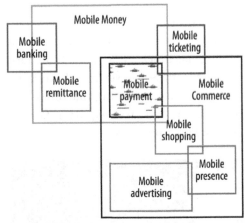

Figure 6-5. Conceptual mapping of content inside a mobile wallet; here, "presence" refers to personal identity (courtesy of Ernst & Young)[4]

Further, consumers find that the most inconvenient thing about items like plastic cards or paper boarding passes is their static nature; they offer no information apart from what is printed on them. A debit card lets consumers buy goods anywhere, but it can't provide feedback on how much money is in their account, or if they are straying from their monthly budget. A paper boarding pass shows a flight's departure gate, but if that gate changes due to the whims of the travel gods, the pass cannot autoupdate; most people have to strain to listen to the many airport announcements to catch the latest updates. These are the types of pain points that we as designers are charged to alleviate and find better

---

4 Ernst & Young, Mobile Payments Report, slide 3, June 2012 (*http://slidesha.re/1qVnIN6*).

solutions for, so that we can ultimately improve consumers' daily lives. These pain points clearly speak to what consumers will expect from mobile wallets: features that are appropriate for the context of their physical location and help them with everyday tasks like shopping and travel.

Managing Mobile Money

In the last decade, banks have been in the midst of a service revolution, similar to what the airline industry went through in the first half of the decade. Users were tired of dated, cumbersome web services, so outsiders like Orbitz and Kayak were able to swoop in with expedited booking flows and engaging, visual approaches to flight searches. These aggregators had simplified the tasks of comparing prices and booking trips, which proved an attractive alternative to users. This type of "experience diversion" is starting to happen in the banking world.

As I wrote in Chapter 1, with the advent of mobile budgeting and banking apps like Mint and Simple, traditional brick-and-mortar banks are finding that their web banking services are being filtered through the glossy sheen of thoughtfully designed and tested new interfaces. Instead of a list of bank statement PDFs and dry account histories with hard-to-read descriptions, Mint users can see pie charts showing their spending patterns within a custom date range (Figure 6-6, left). Instead of typing in the account number and routing number of the landlord to pay the rent with an electronic transfer, renters can use Square Cash (Figure 6-6, right) to send a payment with their debit card just by writing an email.

Users expect that the payments they make with their mobile wallets in the store will be complemented by the types of services banks have always provided: keeping them informed of their available balances, letting them know when they've hit a limit or if fraudulent purchases have been made, and supplying them with a detailed record to review where their money is going. Paper receipts can easily be lost, but a mobile wallet gives users a robust spending history that they can access at any time. Aside from high security standards, banks can add real value to a mobile wallet experience by supplying users with the feedback of real-time financial data. Otherwise, paying with a mobile device is really no different than swiping a card or writing a check.

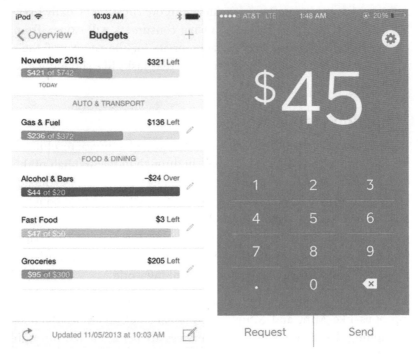

Figure 6-6. Mint's budget charts (left) and Square Cash's ultra-simple person-to-person payments (right)

BALANCES AND TRANSACTION HISTORIES

No customer likes that feeling of trying to pay for something with a credit or debit card that gets declined, certainly not when his fellow shoppers look on with furrowed brows while he fumbles for an alternate card to use. Thankfully, designers can help to avoid this scenario. We can design a home screen, deployed on a connected device, that keeps the user's available balance in plain view (see Figure 6-7). This number could be a running balance or available credit value, and can be shown on or around the image of the card being used. If there are multiple cards in the wallet, this number can help the user select which card to use for a given transaction.

A companion to the available balance is the transaction log, which can show a user how much money she is spending, and where she's spending it. Here, an easy-to-read table with clear typographic hierarchy and scannable values can both act as a confirmation that a mobile payment went through as well as provide transparent activity logs, which can reassure the user that fraudulent payments can be traced.

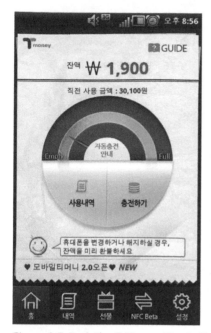

Figure 6-7. Both the T-Money (South Korea) transit wallet and Harris + Hoole (UK) show prominent balances for the user's prepaid cards

Besides card numbers, enormous amounts of metadata can be gleaned from a swipe or a tap in today's mature point-of-sale systems. Each payment a user makes with a credit or debit card is accompanied by more than just the amount; in addition, the following data is captured: the currency used, the name and address of the merchant that took the payment, what kind of store, the date and time of the transaction, whether it was a return, and if so, for how much. You can see some of this data in the receipts displayed in Royal Bank of Scotland's banking app and Google Wallet (Figure 6-8). This data can be used to supply users with rich payment histories that illustrate how and where their mobile money is being spent, and can help them form budgets out of spending patterns. Retailers may also use this data to tailor relevant money-saving offers and coupons that can be sent over the air to the customer's wallet.

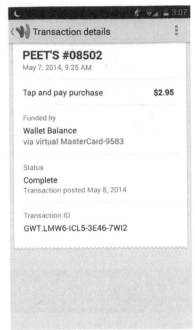

Figure 6-8. The transaction history and digital receipts in the Royal Bank of Scotland and Google Wallet apps provide easy-to-read, robust data about each purchase

BUDGETING

Now that consumers have this data available to them about their mobile payments, what might they want to do with it? After all, it's only telling them about payments that have happened in the past. What about forecasting the user's future spending patterns based on past payment activity? This is an insightful tool that helps users make smart spending and savings decisions. Pivo (Figure 6-9) is a groundbreaking banking app from OP-Pijolo in Finland. The first screen of the experience has a line graph not only of the ups and downs of the user's current and past balances, but also *forecasts* of what the balance may be in the future. Pivo bases this predication on the user's spending patterns, plus any scheduled future bill payments. This kind of visual feedback can have a positive effect on consumer spending habits, discouraging users from living beyond their means.

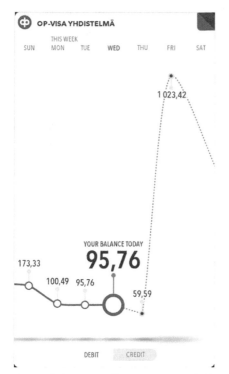

Figure 6-9. Pivo Wallet's innovative balance timeline

Apps that can be linked to a bank account, like Moven and Level (Figure 6 10), have taken a more visceral approach to keeping users in the black. They both employ very simple visualizations reminiscent of fuel gauges to weigh the user's pending payments and available balances. This is great for people who are averse to long tables and graphs, giving them an at-a-glance cue about how much they have left to spend for the month.

Figure 6-10. Moven (left) and Level (right) use very simple yet compelling visualizations to help users stick to their budgets

Among the many human-centered upgrades that Simple has introduced to the banking experience, budgeting is one core component of the app that is done in a way that takes the intimidation out of financial planning. This is great news for people like me, who are not so great at sticking to a financial goal and achieving it.

There always seem to be unforeseen circumstances that get in the way of putting aside money for the future: unexpected car repairs, impulse shopping, spontaneous dinners at fancy restaurants, and so on. Let's say I need to save up about $5,000 to buy a new laptop for my work. With Simple, I can set the amount and time frame I would need to complete that goal (Figure 6-11). With each passing day, Simple will automatically deduct a small amount from my balance (which Simple calls the "Safe-to-Spend" number) and apply it toward the goal I have set.

Figure 6-11. Simple lets users set savings goals and then sets aside small amounts each day to help them achieve those goals

A Mobile Shopping Assistant

When users leave their house to go shopping, they will typically have at least two personal items with them: their wallet and their phone. To date they need their wallet for the cards and cash inside, but how could we utilize the phone to help them shop? One logical supplement to payments is enabling the collection and use of money-saving programs like rewards cards and coupons.

LOYALTY AND REWARDS

Users want more than just "digitized credit cards" from a mobile wallet. In fact, *anything* they might carry in an analog wallet is fair game. In 2012, First Data, a payments processing company, surveyed 4,000 consumers in 11 countries on their shopping and banking behaviors.[5] Of the respondents, 71% expected to be provided with "real-time access" to their bank balance and transaction history. In 2013, market research firm Vibes talked to 1,000 mobile users in the US, and asked them what they would want in a mobile wallet, apart from payment features.[6] Out of this sample, 22% said they would want it to digitize paper items like coupons and loyalty cards, while 13% expected to receive time-sensitive offers based on their spending habits.

When we address these types of consumer needs, we can elevate payment apps from being one-trick ponies to keep users coming back for more. The Starbucks Card app (Figure 6-12) is the most successful mobile wallet of its kind in the US, processing around 3 million

---

5 First Data 2013 Global Universal Commerce Consumer Tracker Study (*http://bit.ly/1qVnTbc*).

6 "2013 Mobile Wallet Consumer Report," Vibes, August 2013 (*http://bit.ly/1qVnZQf*).

transactions a week, as of 2012.[7] Aside from America's love affair with Frappuccinos, the app keeps users coming back in part because it not only lets them carry a reloadable "gift card" in their phone for use at any Starbucks location, but also tracks their purchases and applies them as credits for free drink rewards. Supplemented with features like offers and gift cards that can be sent to friends, the Starbucks app is a perfect example of how to add value to a mobile payment app, extending the experience beyond the spectacle of whipping out a phone to pay for no-whip hot chocolates, and giving users convenient and timely incentives.

Figure 6-12. Starbucks users rack up rewards for free drinks each time they pay

---

7   Kevin Fitchard, "US Mobile Wallet Users Spent $500M in 2012—Nearly All of It at Starbucks," GigaOm, June 4, 2013 (*http://bit.ly/1qVo7ix*).

There are dozens of loyalty apps in the Shopping category of your chosen app store, some by aggregators like Stampt or Belly, and others from merchants themselves, like Target. The most successful loyalty apps tend to have three key elements:

- Ability to search for nearby participating merchants, with links to native maps

- Simplified redemption process, either by tying the rewards to payments, or by showing a barcode/QR code at checkout or "hands-free" via geolocation

- An at-a-glance points tracker visualization, paired with an easy-to-understand rewards system

Loyalty and coupon programs are a favorite channel for merchants, because they want to encourage repeat business. Consumers like them because they can pick up savings in the form of rewards or points, but the catch is that users have to *remember* to bring the loyalty card with them each time they intend to visit their favorite merchant. For this reason, bargain hunters tend to bring loyalty cards with them all the time, just in case. In fact, the average US shopper has five loyalty cards in his wallet.[8] That's a sizable stack of plastic to carry around!

Unlike points earned from credit card purchases, loyalty cards are closed loop systems, so are only redeemable at specific merchants. This led to the advent of form-factor key fobs handed out by grocery stores, or customers enrolling in programs by disclosing their phone numbers, which they enter at the point of sale to get their points. Startups like Shopkick and Belly (Figure 6-13) have found a niche here, creating loyalty programs for many merchants at a time and consolidating them into one app, so that there is no plastic to carry around, and it's easier for consumers to track how many points they have or what rewards they can earn. This proves a compelling reason for users to return to their favorite merchants (and your app) over and over again in order to rack up savings for future purchases.

---

8 Phillip Britt, "5 the Magic Number for Loyalty Cards: Study," Polaris Marketing Research, August 6, 2012 (*http://bit.ly/1qVoeL4*).

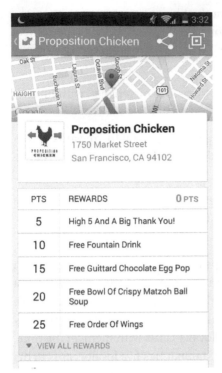

Figure 6-13. Belly, which picked up 2 million users within a year of launching,[9] gives users an easy-to-read tally of points earned, and how far they have to go to hit a reward level

Isis and Google Wallet are ideally placed to simplify the loyalty-card-plus-payment experience, as users can present their cards along with their payment information in one NFC tap. However, Google Wallet falls short of a more complete loyalty experience in that it doesn't consistently tie in a tally of points earned from the user's loyalty programs, and has an awkward redemption flow (Figure 6-14). Isis Wallet does this quite well, presenting any loyalty cards and offers the user has selected in the transaction with one NFC tap. Ideally, loyalty features within a mobile wallet should be executed in a transparent, lightweight manner, no matter the form factor. This allows users to earn savings in an effortless way, and gives them an incentive to use a mobile wallet over a plastic card for this purpose.

---

9   Aaron Tilley, "Customer Loyalty Tech Startup Belly Raises Another $12M from Andreessen Horowitz," Forbes, August 28, 2013 (*http://onforb.es/1qVolq5*).

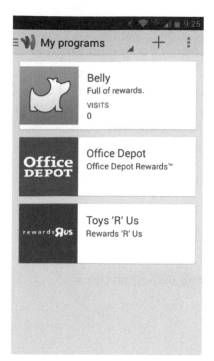

Figure 6-14. Google Wallet lets users add their loyalty cards, but they can get credit for purchases only if they remember to show the barcode to the merchant at the time of purchase, instead of passing the card information along with the NFC payment tap; with the exception of a Belly card, the app doesn't offer reward status or point trackers either

OFFERS AND COUPONS

Merchants have employed offers and coupons for 125 years to get people to walk in their doors; we know the coupon system works.[10] Bargain-conscious consumers tend to love them, so retail brands go out of their way to find more efficient ways to get them into consumers' hands, like getting coupons into mailers, newspaper inserts, and on a stand in store lobbies. Merchants generally strive to make coupons as portable and "redeemable" as possible for consumers—for example, by creating perforated tearouts for coupons, and printing them on the back of purchase receipts.

---

10 Kim Gittleson, "The First Coupon," WNYC.org, June 17, 2011 (*http://bit.ly/1qVoxpl*). One of the first widely circulated coupons may have been in 1887: vouchers for free bottles of Coca-Cola—a five-cent value!

Discovery

Much of the initial development that goes into building an offer experience is put toward content—that is, gathering local and national deals from aggregators or working directly with brands. However, even an app with thousands of name-brand coupons can be rendered useless if the user isn't given an effective means of searching for them. Four mobile location-search best practices are best applied here, including:[11]

- Allow users to search by zip code or current location

- Give users control of search results with both a map and list view

- Let users limit search results to categories they are interested in

- Show meaningful icons or thumbnails on overlays that show the merchant and the deal

Groupon (Figure 6-15) is a great example of these practices.

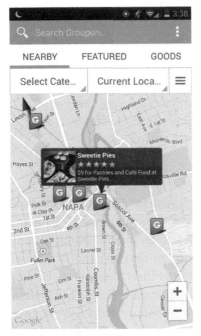

Figure 6-15. Groupon's map for local offers makes searching for nearby offers a snap

---

11 For a fantastic collection of design patterns in this search mode, see Theresa Neil, *Mobile Design Pattern Gallery*, 2nd edition, *http://www.mobiledesignpatterngallery.com/* (Cambridge, MA: O'Reilly Media, 2014).

Redemption

Once users have zeroed in on a deal they are interested in, the detail view should give a very clear description of the offer, when it expires (if applicable), where to find the merchant, and how to redeem it, as seen in Google Offers (Figure 6-16). A well-designed offer screen with a clear and obvious redemption method is much more likely to be used before the expiration date. Here, Google has kept the redemption barcode at the top, so that even if the details and stipulations of the offer run long (as is often the case with coupon marketing content), users won't miss the barcode.

Figure 6-16. Google Offers provides a succinct summary of the offer's attributes, expiration date, where to find the merchant, and the barcode for redemption

Keep in mind that your consumer is not the only user in this scenario; offering details along with a large, easy-to-find promo code will make it much faster for the sales cashier to apply the offer to the purchase. This is evident in Eureka Offers' coupon detail screens (Figure 6-17). Target's new coupon app, Cartwheel, takes this efficiency one step further by binding several coupons to one barcode, which is helpful to both the sales cashier and the customer for applying multiple discounts to one purchase (Figure 6-17).

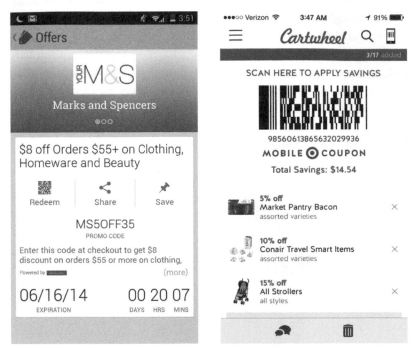

Figure 6-17. Eureka Offers (left) takes the guesswork out of finding the promo code; Target's CartWheel (right) expedites redemption by letting the user link several coupons to a single barcode, so the sales cashier has to scan only once

Context

Mobile is a natural next step for putting savings literally right into the consumer's hands. That means that context is the key to making mobile coupons a strong incentive to use a mobile wallet. While searching for coupons *before* a shopping trip is a common use case, presenting an offer at the exact moment that it's most relevant to users (i.e., when they are in the store with their phone) instantly makes that offer more palatable. It should be no surprise, then, that 63% of users would be more likely to buy something in a store if they were served up a location-enabled coupon as they walk in.[12] A great example of this is when RetailMeNot (Figure 6-18) uses geofencing to send push notifications that tell users when they are near a participating merchant.

Figure 6-18. Geofencing allows RetailMeNot to let users know when good deals are nearby

Personalizing deals

As users browse available deals, apply familiar "favoriting" or "saving" patterns to let them build a repository of offers they are most interested in. If you think about it, this really is just the mobile version of coupon clipping!

This should be as simple as a button that saves a single offer to a My Coupons tab, as seen in RetailMeNot. Mobile wallets should also let users customize the deals they are shown by marking their favorite brands, as Isis Wallet has done in a cutesy manner by letting users "love" a retailer (Figure 6-19, right).

---

12 Lauren Johnson, "Mobile Coupons Trigger 51pc of Consumers to Shop In-Store: Study," Mobile Commerce Daily, June 24, 2013 (*http://bit.ly/1qVoJVr*).

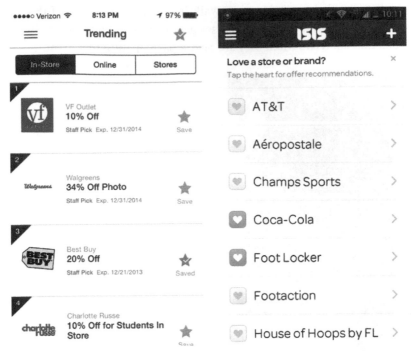

Figure 6-19. Both RetailMeNot (left) and Isis Wallet (right) let users customize offers by indicating their favorite brands or saving deals they'd like to use later

A gestural approach to this interaction can be seen in Eureka Offers, where users drag and drop tempting deals into a "drawer" of saved offers (Figure 6-20). This is a helpful metaphor that impresses upon the user exactly where in the app these offers are saved, so that it's easy to go back and find them for later use.

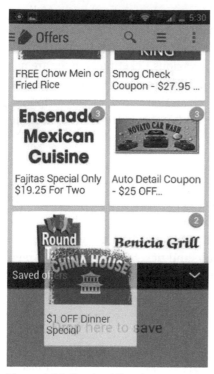

Figure 6-20. Eureka Offers has a Saved Offers drawer, into which users can drag and drop coupons

Mobile Travel

Mobile wallets can also make an impact on streamlining the often-frustrating experience of travel. In this vein, consumers are warming to the idea of using their mobile devices to keep track of their travel plans and boarding passes. SITA, which provides IT infrastructure to the airline industry, surveyed over 2,400 airline passengers across the world in 2013, and found that 58% wanted to get flight status updates on their mobile device, and 66% would be interested in having a mobile boarding pass.[13] A mashup of mobile payments with transit applications is a convenient way for users to manage their journeys from start to finish.

---

13 "Passenger IT Trends Survey 2013," SITA, 2013 (*http://bit.ly/1qVoOse*).

Traveling can be fraught with confusion and misinformation. Airlines and transit agencies are not known for being progressive with technology, and moving between modes (from bus to underground train to elevated train) can be a hassle when the various ticketing systems are not interoperable. Travelers have to be vigilant in finding posted schedules, maps, and arrival time displays at each station in order to know approximately when their flight will depart, or how to get from one area of the city to another on which lines.

With mobile devices, travelers now expect real-time updates on key factors like departures and arrival times. With public transit systems that use smartcards, like London's Oyster card or Tokyo's Suica card, users need to know how much money is left on their cards and have an easy way to reload them. In these areas, mobile wallets are well suited to help users avoid lines at the turnstile and ticket kiosks. They can help the user keep track of paper boarding passes and cards, and generally make the logistics of travel less challenging, regardless of the method used (NFC, barcodes, BLE, etc.).

TRANSIT

NFC has been deployed in transit systems most successfully in places like Japan, South Korea, and Singapore, where millions of passengers can not only tap their phones to get through the turnstile, but also link their bank account to the wallet app for easy card reloads. In 2011, riders using KT's Cashbee mobile transit app (Figure 6-21) to get around Seoul had tapped their phones 30 million times, which works out to about $9.5 million.[14] Instead of users having to wait in line to check the balance of their card or add money, the app automatically reloads the card over the air if the balance drops below a preset limit.

The updated balance of the card is easy to find, and there is a transaction history screen that logs the last 20 rides. NFC is especially nice to have in underground transit stations where data coverage is minimal at best. If a passenger needs the latest train schedule, he can tap his phone on one of the NFC-tagged posters in the station. Passengers can even transfer money to their friends' Cashbee cards by bonking phones together.

---

14 "Korea Blazes Trail for NFC," GSMA, November 2013 (*http://bit.ly/1qVoZ6S*).

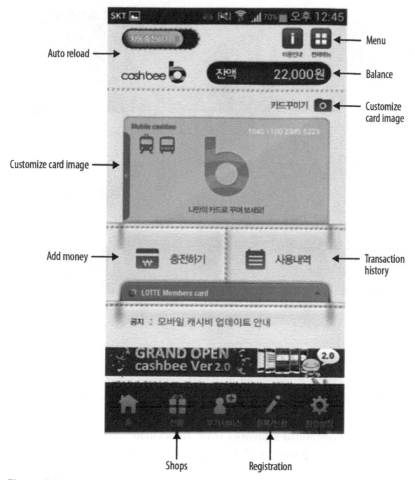

Figure 6-21. KT's Cashbee app lets passengers store a transit card in their phone, which can be reloaded anytime and can even be used at nearby shops

In the US, a few NFC initiatives in transit have sprung up, the most recent being Isis offering free bus rides to trial users in Salt Lake City and Austin. The first was in 2008, when Sprint, First Data, and VivoTech (a POS solutions company) worked together to bring NFC payments to the BART system in the San Francisco Bay Area as part of the EZ Rider program. NFC-enabled phones (Figure 6-22) were handed out to 250 test participants, who could then link debit or credit cards to the device and load up their BART card.[15]

---

15 Ryan Kim, "BART Tries Pay-by-Phone System," *San Francisco Chronicle*, January 30, 2008 (*http://bit.ly/1qVp2zJ*).

Figure 6-22. The BART "EZ Rider" mobile NFC trial in 2008 (photo courtesy of Paul Chinn, San Francisco Chronicle)

Smart posters were displayed in BART stations where users could tap their phones and get directions to the nearest Jack-in-the-Box restaurant, where they could then bring the phone to pay for their meals. After the four-month trial was over, riders had taken 9,000 trips on BART with the phone, and reloaded their mobile BART cards 800 times.[16]

When you are integrating transit services into a mobile wallet, it's best to keep the features lightweight. Passengers will first want to know their transit card balance, so that should be the most prominent, along with a log of recent activity: payments made with the card, and credits from the funding source. If the mobile wallet is enabled with NFC, employ the Tap & Go contactless mode so that the user doesn't have to open the app to tap her phone at the turnstile, for speedier transactions. Ideally, the app should talk to the transit agency's real-time feed of train schedules combined with the device's GPS data to show incoming trains at the station closest to the user (Figure 6-23).

---

16 "BART Trial of Pay-by-Phone Technology Called a Success," BART.gov, October 6, 2008 (*http://bit.ly/1qVpePg*).

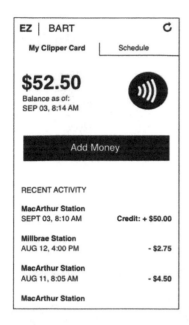
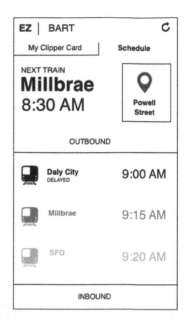

Figure 6-23. An example of transit features within a mobile wallet, which allows passengers to manage their transit card and track incoming trains at nearby stations

AIR TRAVEL

Recently in the world of air travel, airlines have been providing travelers with digital boarding passes via email or within their mobile apps, which the passenger can then show at the gate. This is indicative of efforts within the industry to simplify the airport experience to be more like the transit model, which employs self-service paradigms: passengers check themselves in at a kiosk, find where they need to go, and get where they are going without having to wait in line to talk to an attendant.

A mobile version of the boarding pass is much harder to lose, and the mobile wallet can then act as a concierge throughout the passenger's flight experience, pulling in services like mobile check-in, flight status updates, luggage tracking, and seat requests. A great example of success in this area can be seen in Air New Zealand's mPass app (Figure 6-24), which also shows users their air miles balance and notifies them when a flight is boarding or delayed.

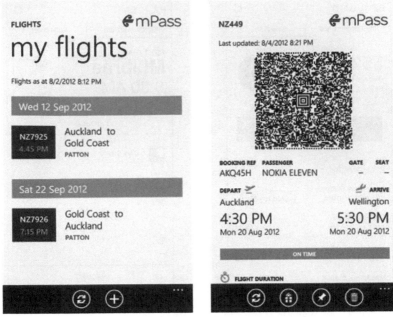

Figure 6-24. Air New Zealand's mPass lets users book and track their flights, and store mobile boarding passes

Apps like Apple's Passbook and Google Now (Figure 6-25) began to support boarding passes from several airlines, such as Air Canada, Air China, Alaska, Virgin Australia, and Lufthansa. A boarding pass linked to the app will pop up on screen right when you need it—as you enter the airport property—and it will be updated with the latest departure gate and boarding times. Within four months of Passbook's launch in 2012, gate attendants at United Airlines were scanning 20,000 mobile boarding passes a day.[17] Of course, Passbook supports other types of ticketing partners, like Amtrak trains, concert tickets from EventBrite, movie tickets from Fandango, and Major League Baseball tickets.

These small revolutions in air travel have caused airlines to take a hard look at the experience design and features of their own mobile apps. United Airlines, in particular, has revamped its iOS app (following Google Now's contextual index card model, with a sprinkling of Windows Metro) so that it can be customized by the user (Figure 6-26).

17 Christina Bonnington, "Apple's Passbook Is a Surprise Success for Developers," *Wired*, December 20, 2012 (*http://wrd.cm/1qVpiio*).

Figure 6-25. Mobile boarding passes in Apple's Passbook (left) and Google Now (right), which provide users with the latest boarding times and flight status notifications

Figure 6-26. The United Airlines app for the iPhone was drastically redesigned as a mobile concierge for passengers

In addition to the boarding pass, users can check in, view their club membership card and points, convert local currencies, swipe through airport maps, and see the weather at their destination.

Summary

People adopt new technology into their lives only when it suits their needs and doesn't get in the way. Fads will fall to the wayside, and true, lasting innovations become subsumed into the daily fabric of mundane tasks that people do in the course of working, living, and playing. And yes, sometimes...shopping.

I strongly believe that the concept of mobile wallets is a prime example of technology solving real-world problems. To undertake the shaping of something that is so personal and unique to the individual using it is no small feat. These aren't easy problems to solve, having so many moving parts and complex ecosystems driving the service environment of the finance, commerce, and travel verticals. That's all the more reason, then, for UX designers and product visionaries to turn their microscope to these services, and see how we can improve and shape them for the near future. I feel that good design should be applied to the everyday with as much fervor as the next big social media startup.

Though here we have touched on a few of the possibilities, there are other areas where mobile wallets can alleviate friction by streamlining processes and content gathering—namely, government services, identification, and healthcare. This is just the beginning!

[7]

Payments on the Horizon

As discussed in Chapter 1, since the dawn of history we have been searching for better and faster payment systems. Each of our innovations was driven by the need to find ways of getting the things we want, using the materials and tools that were available to us at the time. From minting gold coins right up to alternative digital money, quantum leaps in technology have improved the efficiency of daily transactions and changed our spending behaviors.

We can't predict how we will transact in the future. Sci-fi books and movies have occasionally proven to be eerily prophetic, as is the case with the "MultiPasses" used by the characters Korben and Leeloo in 1997's *The Fifth Element* (Figure 7-1). The MultiPass was a handheld cartridge that could be used as an ID, an access key, a travel pass, and a payment card. It had their names, pictures, and medical information on the front, and gold computer chips on the back, which would be inserted into a reader at a reception desk to verify their identities and tickets so they could be granted passage on an intergalactic cruise. Of course, we will set aside that Leeloo's MultiPass (Figure 7-2) was a forgery, and she was actually an elemental being made of pure light.

Figure 7-1. In *The Fifth Element*, Korben and Leeloo presented their MultiPasses (courtesy of Columbia Pictures)

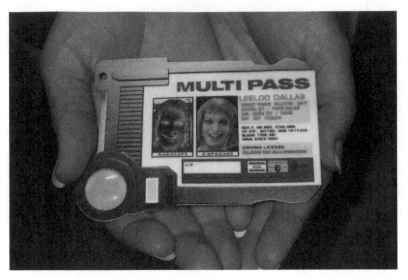

Figure 7-2. Closeup of Leeloo's MultiPass

In the world of *The Fifth Element*, the MultiPass is a contextual tool that can be whatever the user needs it to be in different situations throughout the day. It has the driving clearance that lets the user operate certain vehicles. The bottom frame contains logos for Visa, American Express, and AT&T, so apparently in Leeloo's case, she could use her MultiPass to pay for things, to communicate using the buttons on the frame, or possibly to bill purchases to her phone carrier. Only director Luc Besson knows all the possibilities.

Sound familiar? It's exactly what a mobile wallet could be. The MultiPass predates by a few years the security technology of EMV smart chips, which you can find on new US passports. The technology is widely used for "chip and pin" credit cards in Europe, which will soon become the standard for payment cards in the US. The concept of multiple cards loaded into one form factor—so the user needs to carry only one card—is being explored by the Coin card project (Figure 7-3) The gold chips on the back of the MultiPass may hold the encrypted data of Leeloo's Visa and American Express cards, which is exactly how mobile NFC payments are made possible.

Figure 7-3. Coin allows users to link several credit cards to one "proxy" card, which the user picks from at any time (image courtesy of Coin)

As more innovations come to the fore in the worlds of connected devices and social channels, we will no doubt see their impacts on how we manage and spend our money. Analysts often predict that we will be a cashless society by 2020,[1] and critics of fiat currency usually cite corruption, logistics, and bacterial diseases as reasons to move away from using it. It's beyond the scope of this book to predict what will become of paper money. It could be inferred that the decline of cash may echo the fate of paper checks, the processing of which dropped from 19 billion checks a year in 1995 down to 6.8 billion in 2011, thanks to the popularity of the debit card (and electronic transfers between banks).[2]

The coming years will no doubt bring exciting new paradigms to the payments world, and in the near term, there are already a plethora of nascent technologies and collaborations between the mobile, communications, banking, and payments ecosystems that are leading shoppers in new directions. This new era will have a dynamic cast of characters, which may include:

1 Aaron Smith, Janna Anderson, and Lee Rainie, "The Future of Money in a Mobile Age," Pew Research, April 17, 2012 (*http://bit.ly/1qVyVog*).

2 "Is the Fed Still in the Business of Processing Checks?," Federal Reserve Bank of San Francisco, April 1, 2012 (*http://bit.ly/1qVyZwU*).

- Payment initiatives from tech companies like Apple, Amazon, and Facebook

- Wallets from industry consortiums such as MCX (Merchant Customer Exchange)

- Microcommunication channels like Bluetooth Low Energy beacons

- Authentication with biometrics and gestures

- New form factors like curved displays and wearable devices

This chapter will take a look at some of these players and innovations, with an eye toward how they will fuel challenging new use cases for designers to shape and tailor to the new generation of banking and shopping experiences in the decades to come. As users grow accustomed to these new ways of paying, a typical shopping experience will become more and more effortless. In some ways, this effortlessness will bring us back to the communities of trust we initiated thousands of years ago, where we didn't need coins or cards to purchase goods.

Here Come the 49ers

There's a gold rush in the world of mobile payments right now. Startups like Square and LevelUp (and hopefully readers like you) are taking on the old-guard financial systems with gusto, reinventing the way we shop, pay bills, and send money to friends and family. Like the California Gold Rush of 1849, I expect there will be unforeseen new consumer benefits thanks to this influx of tinkerers, entrepreneurs, and talented outsiders. The 1849 Gold Rush brought us the invention of blue jeans from Levi Strauss (who arrived from Germany intending to make canvas tarps), and helped grow a remote Western outpost into the city that San Francisco is today.[3] With so many new players in the space, consumers will soon have their pick of efficient, user-friendly payment apps.

---

3 One of my favorite stories from this period: when the port of San Francisco became littered with ships abandoned by the waves of hopeful prospectors, city officials decided to salvage the ships to reuse the lumber for municipal building projects and homes. They also sank many of the ships to help create the landfill that scores of startup offices now sit upon in the South of Market (SOMA) district.

APPLE

One player that everyone is watching with anticipation is Apple. Will it adopt NFC like the other mobile platforms, or will it walk its own path? Whichever direction or payment method Apple takes, the majority of consumers will be sure to walk with it.

Apple has placed itself in a unique position, whether it intended to or not, to fundamentally change how and where we shop. The first step was linking users' credit or debit cards to iTunes: Apple now has around 600 million cards on file with this service (and that number's growing every day). This allowed for a funding source for one-tap purchases for apps, music, movies, and books. Next was a way to bridge the gap into tangible retail items.

Apple is known for experimenting with retail technologies within its own brick-and-mortar stores. This is evident in concepts like the Genius Bar appointment system and card acceptance on the sales floor with iPhones (thanks to VeriFone jackets that can process credit card swipes). In 2011, Apple introduced EasyPay (Figure 7-4), which allowed customers to skip the checkout line, to its Apple Store app. A consumer could walk over to the accessories wall, pick up a small item like a set of earbuds, open the app and scan the barcode on the box, touch Pay on his phone, then walk out, receiving a receipt later by email. Frictionless and fun! Then, Apple launched Passbook in 2012 to create a wallet of mobile-friendly coupons, boarding passes, and gift cards. The app uses geolocation to bring up the Passbook item that is most relevant to the user at a given time, like a Target coupon when she drives past a Target store, or a boarding pass for her United Flight as she approaches the airport.

In 2013, Apple took two more steps toward making the iPhone a multi-use wallet. First was the use of Bluetooth Low Energy (BLE)–powered iBeacons (Figure 7-5) placed around its stores. BLE allows for small packets of data to be passed between devices, which is great for concise communications like payments and push notifications (as opposed to the file and music sharing you would do with regular Bluetooth). This allowed for the possibility of setting up multiple fields around the store, each with a different purpose: one welcoming users at the front door, and one in the center aisle informing them of the day's sales or bringing up the EasyPay feature of the Apple Store app to the foreground.

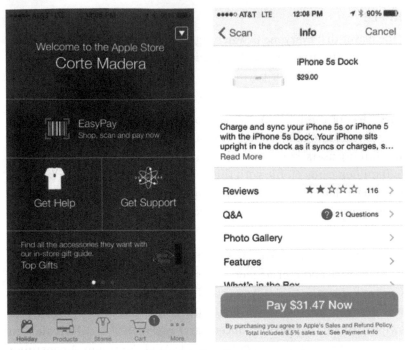

Figure 7-4. Checking out with Apple's EasyPay

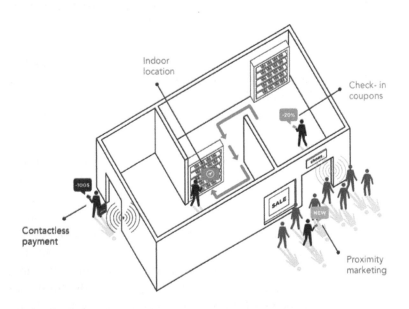

Figure 7-5. How iBeacons could be placed throughout a store to augment a shopping experience (courtesy of Estimote [*http://estimote.com/*])

Beacons were also tested at the Union Square Macy's in San Francisco with Shopkick points, and at Citi Stadium in New York City. The beacons could ping users' phones with helpful content and special offers relevant to their *exact* location, like step-by-step directions to their seats or a coupon for hot dogs if they happened to be near a concession stand (Figure 7-6).

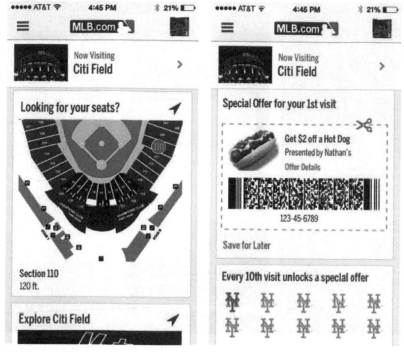

Figure 7-6. iBeacons powered the MLB app with accurate seat finders and coupons that could appear as the user walked past the concession stand (images courtesy of MLB and Mashable)[4]

The second step Apple took was implementing a security and authentication mechanism, unique to each user, which could be used to lock the phone and authorize purchases. That came in the form of TouchID (Figure 7-7), a fingerprint scanner and sensor built into the home button of the iPhone 5S. In 2014, Apple opened the API for TouchID, so

---

4 Samantha Murphy Kelly, "Apple Feature to Turn MLB Stadiums into Interactive Playgrounds," Mashable.com, September 26, 2013 (*http://on.mash.to/1qVz5Vq*).

that apps on the OS could call it to verify the user. This is an obvious authentication factor for banking and payments applications, and Apple made a point to demonstrate it in such a capacity with the Mint app.

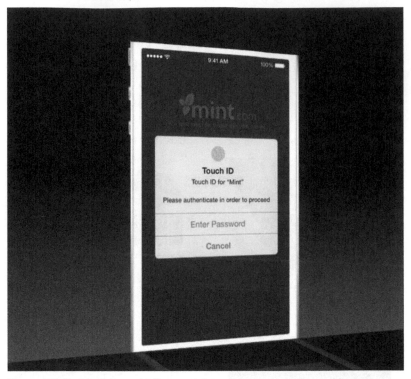

Figure 7-7. Touch ID brought fingerprint scanning to the iPhone, where users could use a finger to lock their phones, to approve purchases in the App Store, or to log in to apps

Hopefully merchants won't overuse channels like BLE to spam visitors to their stores with a bunch of content and offers the customers don't want, as was common practice when SMS alert campaigns and push notifications first entered the mobile scene. But collectively, these features could work within either a merchant's app or an open "iWallet" to deliver an elegant way to shop that is free of all the things that make it not fun—like collecting (and forgetting to bring) paper coupons or loyalty cards, searching for an item in vain, and waiting in long checkout lines. With an Apple-powered wallet, a grocery store trip could look more like Figure 7-8.

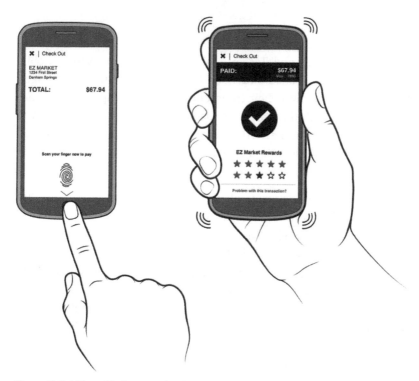

Figure 7-8. When it's time to check out, a user needs only to press his finger on the scanner

Of course, the combination of these features is not unique to Apple. BLE is available in Android phones as of Android OS 4.3, and there are fingerprint scanners being introduced in phones by Samsung, HTC, and Motorola. Still, no one can predict what Apple will do in the space—but whichever transaction method it chooses will surely become the standard, such is its influence on consumer electronics. If Apple adopted NFC in its iPhones or adopted host-card emulation, for example, it would cause a sea change in the payments ecosystem. In the end, between Apple and Google, it comes down to which brand users are more likely to trust with their financial information.

MCX

In 2012, 30 of the largest retailers in the United States—including Gap, Walmart, Best Buy, and Target—banded together to form a mobile wallet consortium called MCX, or Merchant Customer Exchange.[5] Their goal was to lower their transaction costs and capture consumer shopping data with their own mobile wallet solution, as a reaction to NFC wallets such as network operator–led Isis and Google Wallet. Ostensibly, their wallet would be founded on an ethos of good customer service and low barriers to entry.

Not much is known in terms of how the MCX wallet will evolve, but early press releases have revealed that MCX's approach will be based on QR codes and barcodes, which the user would either scan or present at the register to be scanned. Though at first glance this approach does not seem as secure as NFC or cloud wallets, MCX intends to use dynamically generated codes that will change with each new transaction, lowering the risk of unauthorized use should someone steal the user's phone. Each QR code or barcode would "self-destruct" after each payment, requiring a PIN or passcode to generate a new one for the next transaction.

The other possible feature of the MCX wallet is that each merchant may have its own version, so unlike Square or Isis or Google Wallet—which are ubiquitous and can be used at any merchant that accepts them— merchants within the MCX group may have unique wallets, likely containing their coupons and offers, tied to the dynamic QR code/barcode payment mechanism.[6] You could imagine a folder on the user's home screen that looks something like Figure 7-9, if MCX lets merchants dictate their own experiences. However, it is more likely that MCX will be a unified wallet that could work across a selected group of merchants (say, all grocery stores).

---

5   Robin Sidel, "Big Retailers Join Forces to Develop Mobile Wallet," *Wall Street Journal*, August 16, 2012 (*http://on.wsj.com/1qVzgjC*).

6   Dan Balaban, "Gemalto Reveals Some Details of MCX Deal; Vendor Will Earn Fees for Transactions," NFC Times, April 25, 2013 (*http://bit.ly/1qVzlnc*).

Figure 7-9. What a collection of MCX wallets might look like, if each merchant has its own payment apps

Collectively, these 30 merchants bring in $1 trillion in annual sales, and have a long-established base of loyal customers in their pocket. Though this wallet has yet to launch as of this writing, the sheer volume of mindshare that these merchants have with US mobile users makes it a formidable proposition. Again, it comes down to gaining user trust, and incidents like the Target POS breach of 2013 will run long in consumers' memories.

FACEBOOK

Another "silent giant" in the world of payments is Facebook. Like MCX, Facebook has an immense built-in audience, numbering up to 128 million users in the US alone as of August 2013, 101 million of which are mobile users.[7] The company has always fostered some form

---

7 Josh Constine, "Facebook Reveals 78% of US Users Are Mobile As It Starts Sharing User Counts by Country," TechCrunch, August 13, 2013 (*http://bit.ly/1qVzs29*).

of commerce within its network, whether it's buying in-game credits or linked credit cards for Groups to advertise their pages and events. In 2012, Facebook rolled out its Gift feature. Users could browse a catalog of digital and plastic gift cards, which they could then send to friends for birthdays, weddings, or just because. Recipients would get a Facebook message with a redemption code they could use online, or as of 2013, a plastic Facebook Card sent to their home address (Figure 7-10).

Figure 7-10. The Facebook card can hold multiple balances from gift cards

The Facebook Card is reusable, and can hold balances from *multiple* gift cards. For instance, the card could hold "$100 at Sephora, $75 at Target, $50 at Olive Garden, and $8.25 at Jamba Juice."[8] As you receive other gift cards from friends or if you buy them for yourself, the balances are automatically added to your master Facebook Card (Figure 7-11).

This "proxy" model takes the concept of paying for your purchases with reloadable plastic gift cards a bit further than the Starbucks and Dunkin Donuts closed loop cards, where you can use the cards only in the company's store, with its app. Facebook cardholders would be able to reload and manage their cards on the site or in their mobile app.

---

8 "Introducing the Facebook Card: A New Type of Gift Card," Facebook blog, January 31, 2013 (*http://bit.ly/1qVzya7*).

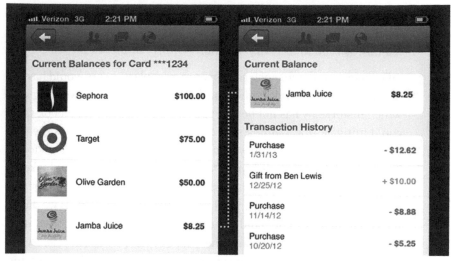

Figure 7-11. Viewing a transaction history for a gift card linked to your Facebook card

Right now, Facebook Cards employ a magnetic stripe on the back of the card, which is provided by Discover. If they went one step further and pulled a Facebook Card barcode or QR code, or linked the multiple balances on the user's Facebook Card to an NFC or cloud checkout, then the user could take the Facebook app and buy things at any of her favorite stores with these prepaid accounts. If Facebook linked the "pseudo-cards" to a bank account or credit card, the balances could be refreshed whenever the user felt like it.

An alternative form of payment via Facebook is purely speculative at this point, but is indicative of how Facebook has come to be our digital representative in the online world, tied to our very real self-identities, and is much more personal than any government-issued ID card. Facebook knows our full names and addresses, where we live, who we talk to, and where we work (that is, if we choose provide those details). That digital identity could be used as currency. If the user has linked a debit or credit card to his Facebook account, and was "checked in" to a nearby shop, then the merchant would need only to confirm who the user is by looking at his Facebook profile picture and name. Once, say, the barista chooses his name from the list of nearby customers, the money for the latte he just ordered can be charged to the debit card he has linked to Facebook, and later the merchant can send him a receipt via email or Facebook message. Facebook's messaging service itself could be a medium for sending payments back and forth between friends, as seen in apps like Venmo.

Of course, in order for such scenarios to take place, users would have to feel comfortable providing their card details to a social networking site, which historically has not been a popular sentiment. A Facebook Card could mitigate this, being a stored-value card that minimizes the risk of users losing a lot of money if their phones were misplaced or stolen. The concept of paying with your "digital-social identity" would take us back to the days when the local shopkeepers were our neighbors and knew our names, families, and where we went on vacation. If we didn't happen to have cash on hand, we could ask the shopkeeper to put it on our tab for payment later, and the shopkeeper was comfortable with that arrangement, knowing our faces and where we lived and trusting us as members of the community.

Emerging Technologies and the Shopping Revolution

Because purchasing things and managing money is something that most of us do every day, it's understandable that we gravitate to co-opting new gadgets and technologies for these purposes. To make a successful purchase, you first need some kind of payment instrument to transfer the funds to the recipient, and you need some way to prove that you are who you say you are and that you have the right to *use* that particular payment instrument. The inventions that seem to work best for commerce are ones that either make our money more compact and portable (coins, plastic cards, mobile phones), or those that allow us to securely and accurately authorize a purchase (pens for signing checks, government-issued ID cards, bill pay with our bank account, debit PINs).

As nascent technologies become conventional payment methods (credit cards, paper money), many are eventually found to be susceptible to some form of exposure or forgery. This is why we look for more secure ways to buy the things we need, but in order for them to be successful, we want security to be balanced with familiarity and ease of use. These two areas (identity security and convenient form factors) have been a hotbed of innovation in recent years, particularly in the use of connected devices and biometrics.

WEARABLE DEVICES

A new wave of everyday items like watches, eyewear, and jewelry has been infused with wireless connectivity, transforming them into wearable smart devices that can feed us information about the world around us, or just enable us to answer phone calls without having to reach into our pocket and pull out a smartphone. If these wearables can be made capable of peer-to-peer communications and linked to the wearer's money, they could easily be used for shopping, to find product reviews, or to do online price comparisons.

One of these fascinating inventions is Google Glass, which frames a small screen in the wearer's peripheral view, and lets him take pictures, get directions, answer calls, or look up things on the Web, primarily with voice controls or gestures. Its use in public has been controversial due to concerns of privacy: some people are concerned that Google Glass owners could surreptitiously record videos of them without their knowledge in restrooms or other private spaces. However, Glass has obvious benefits in several applications where users need a hands-free interface to aid them in finding information quickly (think pilots, mechanics, or surgeons).

Developers have already begun to experiment with how Google Glass could be used for shopping and payments. When Google first announced that Glass would be released to members of the developer community, it had a contest where developers could submit proposals for what they would do with the new device (the prize was a pair of free Glasses). Playground Labs' submission to this contest was a concept video (Figure 7-12) that illustrates how Glass could be a useful tool for shopping, in addition to other use cases like playing video games or learning to play the guitar. The built-in camera could scan the barcode of an item the wearer might want in the store, and perhaps display a table of prices from the store's competitors. At the register, the wearer could use the Glass camera to scan the merchant's QR code to check out, or say "Pay with Credit" to enable Glass to send her card details to the merchant via a nearby BLE beacon. Checking out using Bitcoins is another possibility, as demonstrated by the EAZE app for Glass (Figure 7-13), which lets the user pay with just a nod.

Figure 7-12. User's perspective while shopping with Google Glass (courtesy of a concept video by Playground Inc. [*http://bit.ly/1qVzHKL*])

Figure 7-13. EAZE for Glass, which links to the user's Bitcoin wallet for payments with just a nod of the head

Another new device that could be used for banking and payments is a web-connected watch, like the Pebble, or any of the watches using Android Wear. Resembling something Dick Tracy or James Bond might have used, smartwatches could be used to get bank balances or show a miniature transaction history. In the fall of 2013, Westpac Bank in New Zealand released an app for the Sony SmartWatch (Figure 7-14), which brought the functionality of its CashTank mobile app utilizing one basic function: a visualization of the user's bank balance that was easy to digest at a glance.

Figure 7-14. Westpac's CashTank quick balance smartwatch app

Smartwatches are another handy gadget that is much less conspicuous (and controversial) to wear around, and watches like the Pebble already have a handful of payments apps built into them, such as Pebblebucks (Figure 7-15), which fetches the wearer's last known Starbucks card balance and can show his barcode at checkout. Users can even make payments when the watch is not tethered to their phone, just in case they leave both their wallet *and* their phone at home. The *horror!*

Wearable device experiences typically require minimal physical interaction from the user, often relying on the user's voice or location. In order for payments to be successful with these devices, the act of paying would have to feel natural and seamless. There are unique security problems to tackle with these devices. For example, if your app relies on users entering a passcode before a payment, how would they enter it when there is no keypad to touch? In this case, speaking the passcode to the device would not be ideal.

Figure 7-15. Pebblebucks, a Starbucks payment app for the Pebble smartwatch (courtesy of CNET)

BIOMETRICS

It's important to note that demos of new payment technologies tend to gloss over one inconvenient factor: how users will authenticate themselves to the bank in order to do things like get an account balance or authorize a payment. That is where the second cluster of payment-conducting tech innovations comes in: biometrics.

The problem with current authentication methods is that they are vulnerable to fraud, in various degrees. Signatures are easily replicated, and PINs can be hacked by brute force—that is, attempting all the possible number combinations or known factors (common PINs like 1234 or 2580, or the cardholder's birthdate or address). ID cards can be forged or stolen. Biometrics would greatly reduce the cognitive load that consumers must carry, as their brains are already inundated with PINs, passwords, phone numbers, and addresses. Surveys have shown that 67% of consumers have to remember an average of 11 username and password combinations.[9] When faced with remembering so many disparate security credentials, our human nature tends to lead us to use the same username/password or PIN combinations for different purposes—banking, paying bills, or sending email—elevating the risk of them being compromised. Biometrics would also eliminate the need to carry forms of identification like driver's licenses and passports, as our fingerprints, faces, and voices are unique to each of us. Signing a credit card slip is a thing of the past—not that it's doing us much good now. An anecdote by UK financial technologist Dave Birch illustrates the ineptness of using analog signatures to verify someone's identity: [10]

> Whenever I go to America, and I have to pay with the mag(netic) stripe on the back of the card, I always sign it Carlos Tévez (a famous soccer player)...just as a "security mechanism," so if a transaction ever comes back as disputed and it is signed "Dave Birch" then I *know* it must have been a criminal.

Examples like this are why security researchers experiment with the use of identity hallmarks that are impossible to replicate: parts of the human body.

In the past, true biometrics have been limited to building access and border crossing, or secure laptops and external hard drives that users can unlock with a fingerprint. The hardware needed to scan and read biometric sources like voice inflection, fingerprints, and facial patterns has typically been too expensive and unwieldy to put into the hands of the average consumer or corner store. Mobile devices have, of course, changed this, employing built-in fingerprint sensors, rudimentary facial recognition, and voice passphrases to lock or unlock a device (Figure 7-16).[11]

---

9 "Surveys Show: Consumers Ready to Say Goodbye to PINs, Passwords, and Probing," Nuance, May 8, 2013 (*http://bit.ly/1qVzOWt*).

10 Dave Birch, "Identity in the 21st Century at TEDx Sussex University," May 2012 (*http://bit.ly/1qVzSpm*).

11 Nicole Cozma, "Use Voice Commands from the Samsung Galaxy S3 Lock Screen," CNET, October 15, 2012 (*http://cnet.co/1zYhtuE*).

Figure 7-16. Examples of unlocking a device with voice commands, facial recognition, and fingerprint scans

There have been a few commercial attempts to make biometric scanning at the register a reality, such as pilot programs from Fujistu-backed Pulse Wallet in 2013,[12] which reads vein patterns in shoppers' hands (Figure 7-17), and even a few brief commercial rollouts—like the PayByTouch back in 2002, which let consumers link a bank account with their fingerprint.[13] Most notably, PayPal partnered with Samsung to introduce payment authorization by fingerprint, thanks to the Galaxy S5's scanner (Figure 7-18).

Finnish startup UNIQUL (Figure 7-19) is working on retail kiosks that would allow merchants to use facial recognition to verify customers, scanning them as they approach the register, and claims to reduce checkout times from 30 seconds to 5 seconds.[14] The concept centers on the fact that human faces all have a unique set of metrics when it comes to measuring the distances between facial anatomy. This includes the distance between the eyes, the length of the jaw, the distance from the bottom of the chin to the tip of the nose, and so on.

12 Sajaan Raja, "PulseWallet Offering Biometric POS Transactions with Fujitsu," PaymentEye, November 21, 2013 (*http://bit.ly/1qVzYx8*).

13 Becky Bergman, "Pay By Touch Sees Biometrics as the Key to Secure Transactions," *Silicon Valley Business Journal*, June 19, 2005 (*http://bit.ly/1qVzZRC*).

14 Kunal Aich, "UNIQUL: The Facial Way of making payments," Cool Age, October 18, 2013 (*http://aol.it/1qVA3Rv*).

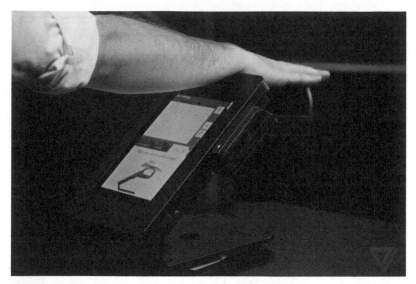

Figure 7-17. PulseWallet attempts to employ biometrics at the point of sale (courtesy of the Verge)

Figure 7-18. PayPal is exploring the use of fingerprint scanners on newer Android phones to authorize payments with a higher level of security than a PIN or password

Figure 7-19. UNIQUL's proposal for a point of sale that would scan customers' faces as they approach to check out

Systems like these are prone to false positives, like when Logan Airport in Boston tested facial recognition at its security gates in an effort to thwart terrorists from sneaking through. Scanning a stream of 40 volunteers each time they went through the security line, the system failed to recognize individuals 38% of the time, likely due to changes in ambient light and the inability to map out the faces of people in motion or at different angles from previous scans.[15]

For designers, biometrics present new challenges in interaction design, especially around instruction and feedback. Designers must provide clear instructions to users on the best angle or direction to swipe their

---

15 Shelley Murphy and Hiawatha Bray, "Face Recognition Devices Failed in Tests at Logan," *Boston Globe*, September 3, 2003 (*http://bit.ly/1qVA8oc*).

finger in order to get a good read on the scanner. Animations and sounds should be incorporated to let users know when their face or voice has been recognized for a payment authorization.

Summary

These innovations, while being huge leaps forward in terms of augmenting our daily lives, raise questions about a variety of issues. Should we allow companies like Apple to see all the things we buy? Should Google Glass wearers be allowed to use them while driving, given the temptation to watch silly YouTube videos rather than focus on the road? Should our grocery stores keep a database of their shoppers' faces and palms? What happens if their database of customer biometric data is compromised or stolen, and customer identities are used for nefarious purposes? It's one thing to have your debit card or your mobile phone stolen, but you only have one face, after all.

These are the types of questions that designers should ask themselves before taking on projects in new tech mediums. The potential for faster purchases may come at the price of exposing consumers to irreparable harm, which is something that we should avoid at all costs. Until the day comes when a 100% impenetrable payment instrument comes along, we must take care never to expose our users' financial privacy in the course of interface design, and enable consumers to be in complete control of their money—no matter how or where they choose to transact.

Companies, Products, and Links

It seems that each week there is a new payment startup or announcement of a mobile initiative from financial institutions. It can be challenging to keep up with it all! The following list of products and companies that are referenced throughout this book, are examples of the emerging design patterns and service design benchmarks that are establishing a new world of mobile commerce and banking interactions.

As this space so dynamic, this list by no means exhaustive and may be outdated as of this printing. For an updated list, please visit the Errata section for this book on the O'Reilly website: *http://bit.ly/ mobile-payment-ex*.

COMPANY	PRODUCT	URL
AT&T, T-Mobile, & Verizon	Isis	*http://www.paywithisis.com/*
ATX Innovation	TabbedOut	*http://www.tabbedout.com/*
Apple	Easy Pay	*https://itunes.apple.com/us/app/ id375380948?mt=8*
Apple	Passbook	*https://www.apple.com/iphone-5s/ built-in-apps/*
Barclaycard US	bPay	*http://www.bpaymobile.com/*
Belly	Belly	*https://www.bellycard.com/*
Biyo (formerly PulseWallet)	Biyo Wallet	*http://biyowallet.com/*
Blackhawk	GoWallet	*https://www.gowallet.com/*
Clinkle	Clinkle	*https://www.clinkle.com/*
Coin	Coin	*https://onlycoin.com/*
Coinbase	Coinbase	*https://coinbase.com/*
Cover	Cover	*http://www.paywithcover.com/*
Dash Software	Dash	*http://dashwith.me/*

EAZE	EAZE Wallet	https://paywitheaze.com/wallet
Kuapay	Kuapay	https://www.kuapay.com/
Dunkin Donuts	Dunkin Donuts Mobile App	http://www.dunkindonuts.com/app
Google	Wallet	https://www.google.com/wallet/
Groupon	Groupon	http://www.groupon.com/
Gyft	Gyft	http://www.gyft.com/
Harris & Hoole	Harris & Hoole Mobile App	http://www.harrisandhoole.co.uk/app
Intuit	Mint	https://www.mint.com/
Iugu	Iugu	http://iugu.com/
Merchant Customer Exchange	MCX	http://www.mcx.com/
LG U Plus	Paynow	https://upaynow.uplus.co.kr/index.do
MasterCard	PayPass	http://www.mastercard.com/corporate/ mobile-paypass.html
Movencorp	Moven	https://www.moven.com/
NTT DoCoMo	Osaifu- Keitai	https://www.nttdocomo.co.jp/english/ service/convenience/osaifu/
O2, Telekom & Vodafone	mPass	http://www.mpass.de/
One Louder	Eureka	http://onelouder.com/eureka
OP-Pijolo	Pivo	http://www.pivolompakko.fi/
PayPal	Here	https://www.paypal.com/webapps/mpp/ credit-card-reader
PayPal	Wallet	https://www.paypal.com/webapps/mpp/ pay-in-stores
RetailMeNot	RetailMeNot	http://www.retailmenot.com/
Safaricom	M-PESA	http://www.safaricom.co.ke/ personal/m-pesa
Shopkick	Shopkick	http://www.shopkick.com/
Simple	Simple	https://www.simple.com/
SCVNGR	LevelUp	https://www.thelevelup.com/
Sony	FeliCa	http://www.sony.net/Products/felica/
Square	Cash	https://square.com/cash
Square	Order	https://squareup.com/order

Square	Register	https://squareup.com/sell-in-store
Starbucks	Starbucks Mobile App	http://www.starbucks.com/coffeehouse/mobile-apps
Target	Cartwheel	http://cartwheel.target.com/
Uber	Uber	https://www.uber.com/
Venmo	Venmo	https://venmo.com/
Visa	payWave	https://developer.visa.com/paywavemobile

[*Index*]

[*About the Author*]

Skip Allums is a UX Lead at Monitise, one of the largest mobile banking and payments technology companies in the world.

A former library scientist, Skip entered the payments world as a true consumer advocate, challenged with designing elegant user experiences for technologically complex mobile transactions. This book is a product of four years of groundbreaking work in the mobile payments space.

CPSIA information can be obtained at www.ICGtesting.com
Printed in the USA
BVOW11s0111080814

362145BV00001B/1/P